A Second Treasury of Magical Knitting

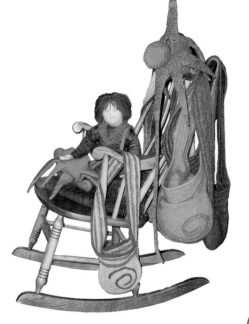

by

Cat Bordhi

ALSO BY CAT BORDHI

A TREASURY OF MAGICAL KNITTING
Passing Paws Press, 2004

SOCKS SOAR ON TWO CIRCULAR NEEDLES: A MANUAL
OF ELEGANT TECHNIQUES AND PATTERNS
Passing Paws Press, 2001

TREASURE FOREST, FIRST BOOK OF THE FOREST INSIDE TRILOGY
WINNER OF THE NAUTILUS AWARD FOR BEST YOUNG ADULT FICTION, 2004
Namasté Publishing, 2003

ISBN 0-9708869-8-5

Book design & layout: Cat Bordhi, in consultation with Bruce Conway
Book cover: Bruce Conway

Photography:
Photos of Vanessa Rose Ament (adult model), empty cat beds, Felted Foursome and Nesting
Moebius Trio, wallet with hands on page 25, Jester Tentacles Bag on page 16, and photos on
pages 10-13, 26-32, 35-36, 38-39, and 109-111 by Michael Hopkins (mahphoto@comcast.
net); Mesmersizing Half-Moebius Mishap on page 78 by Bruce Conway, dewdrops on leaf
in Moscow forest on page 16 by Nikolay Lavrentev; photo of cat teaching on page 108 by
Christopher T. Anderson of Knitopia; all other photos by Cat Bordhi.

Passing Paws Press, Inc.
P. O. Box 2463
Friday Harbor, WA 98250

Email: cat@catbordhi.com
Web site: www.catbordhi.com

Printed in Manitoba, Canada, by Friesens

DEDICATION

As I've been moving between my needles and computer during the long gestation period of this book's birth, it has been the intimate presence of your radiant heart and lively hands, dear knitter, that has inspired me, like the glow of a lamp that is always on.

I feel you beside me, sharing my awe as the Moebius magic unfurls before us, illuminating pathways we didn't know existed.

I've recorded everything in this book for both of us to turn to if we ever forget the sheer wonder of our discoveries.

THANK YOU

 I'd like to tell you a secret. This book was easy. It took a long time, hundreds upon hundreds of hours of meticulous tweaking of graphics, writing, revising, knitting, reknitting, picture-taking, checking off to-do lists that grew longer every day, and teaching workshops where knitters gave me precious feedback on evolving designs. I slept two hours less than normal, fueled by the pure joy of shepherding the book along. And in the midst of this flurry of activity, the book grew peacefully. No matter how much there was to do, at any given moment, what there was to do in *that* moment was easy.

Bruce Conway, my friend and book design guru, taught me to love how white space holds text and graphics in quiet arms, and to see when it is "true." The same tender, silent white space surrounds you and the contents of your mind right now, as quiet and untroubled as the white space holding the words and small photo on this page.

Many beings entered the white space of this book to enrich it. Vanessa Rose Ament, my adult model, and Alyssa, my child model, grace the pages with their radiance. Unicorn, Skacel, Cascade, Crystal Palace, Philosopher's Wool, Russi, and Fleece Artist all supported my discoveries with donations of their beautiful yarns. Gifted Hands and Knitknacks gave me sets of their hand-crafted needles to photograph in the Needle Cozies. You'll find contact information for all in the appendix. I cherish the community of workshop students and knitters who I meet via email or in

person, and feel the pulse of our common heart. Julie, owner of Island Wools near my home, seemed always to have the yarn for knitting my dreams of the night before. My friend Kim sailed over from Lopez Island again, needles and pen in hand, to help proof the book, and then we spent the evening knitting and felting magical Needle Cozies. My friend Callie and her Appaloosa, Miss-Te, agreed cheerfully to my slightly wacky request to model a bit of Moebius magic.

It has been unspeakably thrilling to have non-knitters fall under the spell of magical knitting. My friend Antoinette Botsford, a storyteller of international repute, became uncharacteristically speechless when I put a Trifold Bowl into her hands. Regaining her voice, she whispered, "It gives me the shivers! I'm holding something spiritual." We have plans for knitting lessons. I met Robert Lang, an origami master and author of many books on the subject, when he was being honored at an art show on the intersection of art and math. He is the only person I have ever met who instantly recognized the pathways I followed to knit even the most complex pieces, and he kindly gave me some advice on how I might approach a knitted Klein bottle (two reflecting Moebii joined along their single continuous edges) so that it is as true to its pure form as possible. He ought to know; he folds origami Klein bottles with one sheet of paper, no cuts.

And finally, I could not have written this book so easily were it not for my kind, wonderful, and much-loved daughter and business manager, Jenny, whose consummate organization and financial good sense allow me to concentrate on knitting, teaching, and book-making.

Table of Contents

I really didn't believe that my marker could possibly travel around and show up back here between my needles. But it did.

Magical Knitting Workshop student, Anacortes, Washington

INTRODUCTION & FIRST LESSON

Welcome to the second collection of magical knitting, a fountain of playful and practical designs. As the Moebius stream carries you and your knitting along, you may feel like the friend who wrote to me and compared magical knitting to the graceful sensation of walking the famous labyrinth of Chartres Cathedral in France.

I love watching knitters' faces change during my workshops. Most beginners start out looking a little anxious. Then the magic reveals itself on their very own needles, glowing smiles dawn around the room, and we settle into a day of child-like delight. Here's an important secret: magical, or Moebius, knitting, may not be easy to understand initially, but *there is absolutely no need to.* Like the lilies in the field who need not toil or spin to be so beautiful, you are likely to find that you need only enter the world of magical knitting to enjoy its blessings.

The designs in both books begin with the mysteriously twisted loop you see to the right, called a Moebius band. If you follow my directions for making a paper Moebius, you will instantly experience the mysteries of this form.

At the end of this chapter, I'll teach you to knit a Moebius scarf, since all the magical designs grow from this basic structure.

Please find paper, a pen, scissors, and tape. Cut a long strip of paper. Write *I love to knit,* starting at the bottom left corner of the strip, staying right along the bottom edge.

Hold the ends of the strip together so they resemble a ring.

Carefully turn one end over so the "wrong side" meets the "right side." Tape the ends together.

Now add 'because" to your sentence, and keep writing reasons you love to knit until something stops you. Make sure to write along the *lower* edge, not in the middle of the strip.

ABRACADABRA

How many sides are left on what only moments ago was the familiar two-sided paper you've taken for granted all your life? Examine the *edge* of the twisted ring. Your long sentence reveals that not only have the original paper strip's two sides merged to become one side (one surface), but the two long edges are now one twice-as-long edge.

I think what you've just done is a lot easier than pulling a white rabbit out of a hat, and just as astonishing. You are holding a magical Moebius band, and are about to knit one. In magical knitting, every stitch rotates into position between your needles, even though at first you won't believe it. You knit the stitch between your needles … then knit the next stitch between your needles. It sounds utterly simple, and it is.

You'll learn the simple Moebius Cast-On in this chapter. Read through the scarf pattern that follows, and I hope you'll knit one. After that, you're ready to choose any design in this book, or in the first *Treasury*. And if you're curious to know the origin of the Moebius, you can read all about it in the first *Treasury of Magical Knitting*.

A COMMON MISUNDERSTANDING

A great many knitters still believe that if you make the mistake of twisting the stitches when joining a circular cast-on, the result is a Moebius. This is not the case. This twisted line of stitches, joined and knit upward, clearly has *two* separate edges – one cast-on (the bottom) and one bound-off (the top). A Moebius has only *one* edge. In addition, this sorry piece of knitting will be found to have two sides, twice as many as the mysterious Moebius. It also has a 360° (full) twist instead of a Moebius 180° (half) twist. And it will not fall very gracefully, with such a lot of twist.

Other knitters are content to knit a long rectangle and graft the ends together to make a Moebius. Unfortunately, they miss out entirely on the delightful knitter's playground of the one-fell-swoop Moebius you will learn here. For when you knit a Moebius in one continuous flow of stitches, beautiful patterns emerge naturally and symmetrically from the center out, with little effort or attention on your part.

But most of all, and this is hard to explain, there is such a feeling of innocence and all-is-well-with-the-world in allowing the true Moebius to do all the work for you. It's the most generous form of knitting I know. You can find this out for yourself, by knitting one.

THE MOEBIUS CAST-ON (MCO)

The Moebius Cast On you are about to learn may be the fastest cast-on in the world, once your hands learn the simple moves. In my workshops I like to demonstrate it behind my back just to let people know that it is pretty easy. Last time I did this I also stood on one foot!

A long circular needle between 47" and 60" long is necessary for knitting the designs in this book. Addi Turbo needles, both metal and bamboo, are available in these lengths, Crystal Palace bamboo needles come in a 55" length, and you can purchase a Denise Needle Kit with additional longer cables to give you all the sizes you need to knit everything in both *Treasuries*. Your knitting may be a bit slower with Denise needles because the cable is thicker and less pliant, but if you use a smaller tip for the left needle, the stitches will flow along very nicely, and your gauge won't be affected (only the right needle tip determines gauge).

You need such a long needle because it works in a coiled position, like the needle shown here:

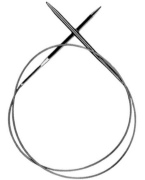

There's enough cable on this 47" needle to allow the tips to interact easily.

The needle tips must to be able to work together, and shorter needles simply do not offer enough cable length to allow easy work.

TWO BASIC MOVES TO REPEAT
- Scoop a loop from *under* the cable.
- Scoop a loop from *over* the cable.

The photos show the step by step process.

SET UP
Make a slip knot and place it near one end of the cable, as shown. The needle closest to the slip knot hangs

down and is ignored until you have finished casting on. The other needle does the casting-on. Note that the needles are pointing in *opposite* directions.

HOME POSITION
Here is how you hold the yarn, cable, and needle. Your right thumb and middle finger pinch the

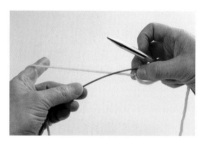

slip knot and cable. Your right hand also holds the working needle. The yarn runs *behind* the cable and is tensioned in your left hand. Your left thumb and middle finger pinch the cable.

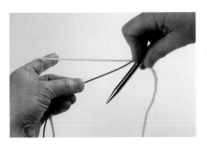

STEP ONE
Here we go.
The needle dips
down in *front* of
the cable.

STEP TWO
The needle
goes *under* the
cable and comes
up inside the
triangle between
the cable and
the yarn.

STEP THREE
The needle rises
up from the
triangle.

STEP FOUR
The needle
swoops *over*
the top of the
yarn and down
behind it, ready
to scoop a loop
and bring it "home."

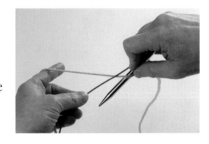

STEP FIVE
The needle has
scooped a loop
and is bringing
it back *under* the
cable, retracing
its earlier path,
"home" to the
space between you and the cable
(as shown on page 10, "Home position").

STEP SIX
The needle
reaches up over
the top of the
yarn, ready to
scoop a loop.

STEP SEVEN
The needle is
scooping a loop.
Notice it has
reached up, *over*,
and behind the
yarn to scoop
the loop.

STEP EIGHT
The needle has
retraced its path
and is bringing
the scooped loop
"home."

COUNTING MCO STITCHES

Now that you've practiced the MCO, I'll teach you how to count your stitches correctly, and have you practice the MCO once more while you count out loud. *Count each scoop as one stitch.* Notice that for every two stitches you scoop, two matching stitches appear on the cable be-

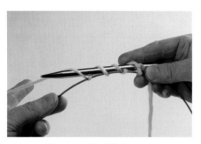

Here are 4 stitches

neath the needle. You will be knitting these lower stitches, but *do not count them when you cast on* or you will end up with half as many stitches as you need! Only count the scooped stitches, which are on top. See the four stitches on the needle? These are the stitches you count – they are the loops you scooped. Do *not* count the slip knot you began with.

CHECK FOR ONE CROSSING BY GOING FOR A TRAIN RIDE

It is essential that you check to see there is just one crossing of cable and needle, as shown by the arrow. Spread the stitches so they reach from one needle to the other as shown here. You will have to pull or push the cables, needles, and stitches to get them into position.

Think of the cables and needle as a train track. If a train is to travel these tracks, they must be parallel, like the l's in the middle of the word, parallel. Starting with *one crossing of the right needle and the cable*, as indicated by the arrow in the photo in the bottom left corner (either needle over cable, or cable over needle), press the cables flat and parallel all the way around to the left needle. Rotate the left needle back around the cable if necessary, until the train track is parallel from the single crossing all the way around. It is rare to have more than one crossing, but you must always check to be sure. I learned the hard way! (The needles do cross one another, but this is irrelevant.)

KNIT YOUR FIRST STITCH

Now place a marker on your right needle (my marker is beaded). Insert your needle through the loop of the slip knot and knit this first stitch.

JUST SAY NO TO THOSE LEAPING FROGS

On the first round, when you try to push the stitches up the left needle so they can be knit, the stitches tend to leapfrog over one another and make it hard to slide them along. Spread the crowded stitches apart and push them up the needle one at a time. The first half round *is* awkward, because the cast-on stitches are wiggly. After the first half round is completed, the stitches will be stable and move along nicely.

FIRST HALF ROUND

On the first half round, the stitches are mounted alternately, so that you must knit one through the back leg, the next through the front leg, and so forth.

Knitting into the back leg of a stitch.

Knitting into the front leg of a stitch

SECOND HALF OF ROUND

Continue knitting alternately through back and front legs until you find your marker dangling on the cable *beneath* your needles, *where it cannot be removed* (see below). You are halfway around the single continuous edge. From this point on the stitches will all be mounted normally. You may notice purl bumps along the entire needle and be quite sure you have knit one full round – but actually you are only halfway around. Take a look and you'll see there are no purl bumps on the other side of the needle yet. Soon there will be.

THE NEXT STITCH

Knit into the stitch formed by the side of the slipknot. The slip knot itself is looped around the cable to the right of the marker.

ONWARD

Continue knitting until the marker finally appears in between your needles, where it could fall off if you aren't careful. Notice that now there are purl bumps on both sides of the needle all the way around. *When a pattern says, "knit to the marker," it means knit until the marker appears* between *your needles, not on the cable below.*

You have completed your first round. You may see a bit of a gap beside your yarn tail. Once you've completed the project you will use the tail to weave the gap together. As for the slip knot, in all the Moebii I've knit, I have never once noticed the knot in a finished piece, and you probably won't either.

Do you see how the knitting is widening between your needles? Believe it or not, you are knitting your Moebius band from the "spine," or center line, out. Each time you complete one round, two rounds of stitches show up between the parallel cables. If you were to suddenly change colors, you would have a stripe on both sides of the spine after completing one round. You have entered the dimension of magical knitting.

YOU'RE READY TO BEGIN

At this point you have the skills to begin your first project. For a while, you will probably wonder what you are doing and how it will turn out. Don't worry. To succeed, you only need to knit each stitch as it rotates into place between your needles. And every stitch will arrive, endlessly and in perfect sequence, until it is time to bind off. There are no forks in the simple road of magical knitting, so you cannot take a wrong turn. You're home safe.

Your First Moebius

This beginner's Moebius scarf welcomes you to the simple and mysterious dimension of magical knitting. It will fit your shoulders like a stream of water rounding a smooth stone, and drop gracefully into a pool on your bosom before streaming back up and around your shoulders in a never-ending embrace.

The delicious nubby hand-painted silk yarn from Fleece Artist in Nova Scotia has a lovely drape and texture. And as I knit with this silk, it made tiny little sounds that instantly transported me into my childhood, back to the enchantment of riding a pony with a squeaky leather saddle. Feel free to knit this scarf with any yarn, or combination of yarns held together, that will give you about the same gauge.

For an extensive collection of Moebius scarves, from simple to lacey, shaped, striped, chevroned, or lightly felted, see my first Treasury of Magical Knitting**,** *where you'll also find many patterns for magical Moebius footwear, capes, wraps, and hats.*

Yarn: Fleece Artist Hand Dyed Silk Spun (100% silk, 100 g/ 150 m, 10 wpi), 1 skein

Needles: (you may require a different size to get correct gauge) size 10 (6mm) circular, 47" - 60" length

Notions: tapestry needle, stitch marker

Gauge: 10 sts = 4" (10 cm)

Finished size: 9" width (stretched), 46" circumference

Stitch guide: See page 112 for abbreviations. Refer back to pages 10-13 for technique illustrations and explanations.

Beginning

MCO 115. Check to be certain there is just one crossing of needle and cable, place a marker on the right needle tip, and then knit your first stitch, the slip knot. For the first half round the stitches will be mounted alternately, so be sure to knit them through the back loop, then the front loop, etc., (see page 13). When your stitch marker appears between your hands again, notice that it is not on the needles, but on the cable below, where it cannot be removed. This signals that you have completed the first half round of the long continuous Moebius edge. The first stitch of the next half round is on your left needle tip now, formed by the double sides of the slip knot as it loops down around the cable below. Knit it as if the double sides are one strand. You'll find that from now on all the stitches are mounted correctly. Continue knitting until your stitch marker reappears in between your needles (see page 13), where it announces that you have completed your first full round. From now on, every time you see the marker between your needles (not on the cable below), you will know you have knit one complete round.

Middle

Knit 7 more complete rounds - which means that the marker will appear in *between* your needles 7 more times. Notice how all knitting (no purling) results in a pattern of stockinette above the spine and reverse stockinette below. This a bit of Moebius magic. Purl 8 complete rounds (the marker appears between your needles 8 times). See how all purling results in reverse stockinette above and stockinette below? More magic! Knit 4 complete rounds (the marker appears *between* your needles 4 times). Perhaps you predicted what would happen when you resumed all knitting - you have stockinette above and reverse stockinette below. Over time you will learn to predict what a Moebius will do.

Edge

The scarf is bound off with an applied I-cord edge, which is used in patterns throughout this book. I think you'll love the way it looks. Cast on 3 sts as shown on page 110 and follow the directions for applied I-cord, working until all sts are bound off. Then either bind off the I-cord and sew the ends together, or graft the unbound end to the beginning end as shown. Weave in all ends.

Blocking

As I mentioned in the first *Treasury*, it is not possible to lay a Moebius scarf continuously on any surface in your house, nor on any surface you could construct in the dimension we live in. If you want to block the scarf, try placing a folded towel over the end of an ironing board and draping the damp Moebius over the towel so the half-twist hangs below. You may want to rotate it now and again so that all surfaces have an equal opportunity to lie flat for a while.

Yarn and design suggestions

If you'd like a Moebius scarf in a different gauge, circumference, or width, it's easy. Simply knit a gauge swatch in stockinette. Then multiply your stitches per inch by the desired circumference to obtain the MCO number. For instance, a scarf with a 50" circumference knit at a 4 stitches per inch gauge would require 4 x 50 = 200 stitches for the MCO. Review page 12 for how to count MCO stitches. How many stitches you cast on determines the *circumference*, or *length*, of your scarf, while the number of rounds you knit determines the *width*. You simply knit until your scarf is wide enough, then finish the edge.

A Moebius scarf is a wonderful way to use up your stash, especially if you combine yarns. I have yet to find a yarn that doesn't want to become a Moebius scarf! You can vary the width of the purl and knit rounds, or even knit every single stitch, creating a scarf with thick rolled edges. Take a look at the first *Treasury* to whet your imagination, and embark on an exciting adventure of experimentation.

I've just thought of a thousand ways to use my stash . . .
overheard at a Magical Knitting trunk show

CHAPTER ONE - ANCIENT FIBER MAGIC

Felt may be the most ancient of all fabrics, requiring only wool (straight off the sheep, or plucked here and there from thorn bushes), water, and a pair of hands to massage the fibers until they matt. For thousands of years, we humans, born without fur or feathers, have sheltered ourselves from the elements with felted footwear and clothing, slept in felted blankets, and even lived in small homes made of felt.

If you have never tried felting, beware! It's a rare knitter who can be satisfied with just one felting adventure. You may find yourself under the spell of a new obsession.

Most, but not all, of the designs in this book are felted. The unfelted designs include the flexible Shape-du-Jour Moebius Baskets, the Moebius scarf in the previous chapter, and unfelted sling bags, knit of plant fibers.

Sometimes people who haven't felted before hesitate to allow their knitting to undergo such an irreversible and mysterious transformation. Don't be afraid. The worst that can happen is that your piece will turn out too small, and I'll teach you how to avoid this. In other words, you can't go too far wrong. Start with a small project, like a Needle Cozy or a Moebius Basket, and discover what felting is all about.

SIMPLE STEPS OF FELTING

• Knit with a looser gauge and in a larger size than you want to end up with.

• Agitate it in a washing machine with hot water and a little soap, until felted.

• Spin or press dry, then refine by pushing and patting into desired shape.

AND NOW IN MORE DETAIL ...

Only animal fibers will felt

You must choose wool, alpaca, llama, angora, mohair, cashmere, or a blend of animal fibers, to produce felted fabric. Synthetics do not felt, and if an animal fiber label indicates it can be machine laundered, it also will not felt.

Knit to a relatively loose gauge

The knitted fibers must be free enough to sway and swim in the warm water, reaching their little hairy fingers out to cling to other little hairy fingers. If you knit with needles several sizes larger than recommended on the label, your gauge will be suitable.

Into the washing machine

Use a low level, hot water setting, and add just a little bit of soap - perhaps a quarter of what you'd use for doing laundry. Add something to help bat the knitting around - a pair of jeans, a half-dozen tennis balls, or some old tennis shoes.

Set the washing machine for low water and the longest agitation cycle, and be sure to set a timer. You'll need to check on the progress of the felting as often as every minute or as little as every ten minutes, depending on the project. The felting instructions in each pattern will tell you if you need to check especially often.

I use so little soap that I usually don't even bother rinsing. If you do rinse, do so with warm water, as a sudden temperature change will make your knitting suddenly shrink more (which may be desirable, so use a cold rinse if you want to tighten things up). Be careful not to let warm rinse water agitate for more than about one minute, or it will continue to shrink the knitting.

I nearly always spin dry my felted projects. However, there is the possibility that this will felt a crease into the felt. To avoid a crease, stop the spinning once a minute and rearrange the piece. Alternatively, you can press out most of the water with dry towels.

Shape the felt to your taste

After finishing the machine part of the felting process, you will refine the shape and size of the piece. You can tug, press, push, and pat smooth, or even block round pieces using specialized equipment: balloons and inner tubes! If you are making a bowl or basket, blow up a balloon inside it. Pop the balloon after the piece is dry, and it will block to a lovely round shape. I block the large cat beds by inserting a wheel barrow inner tube and inflating it to size. The only draw back is that people look at you funny when you arrive at the service station to blow up your knitting.

PROTECT YOUR WASHING MACHINE

Felting releases lots of loose fiber, and too much of it may eventually gum up the workings of your machine. To protect against this, put the knitted piece inside a pillowcase and seal the top with a very strong rubber band. If you're going to do a lot of felting, I recommend that you sew a cloth bag with a heavy-duty zipper (an ordinary zipper will burst open), which allows easy checking during the felting process. Felting inside a pillowcase also protects your project from soaking up other fibers that may be floating around in your washing machine, which could embed themselves in the felt.

ALTERNATIVES TO A WASHING MACHINE

An ordinary top-loading washing machine can be opened to monitor the felting progress, and may also be reset to repeat the wash cycle as many times as desired without wasting water. If you do not have this kind of machine available, and your local laundromat has only front-loading machines (most of which do not allow you to interrupt the cycle), here are several old-fashioned, somewhat silly, yet practical alternatives.

Plunger method

Buy a clean plunger, the kind used to unstop a toilet. Fill a deep sink or large bucket with warm soapy water, and work that plunger up and down until your knitting is felted just the way you want. An advantage to this method is that you can see what's happening at all times.

Wild child method

A bathtub or outdoor wading pool filled with warm soapy water and exuberant children will produce enough agitation to felt your knitting. You must, of course, stand by at all times as lifeguard and to determine when to rescue your knitting from the chaos.

Musical washboard method

Rubbing your warm, wet knitting across the ridged surface of an old-fashioned washboard allows you to selectively felt certain areas more intensively. This is useful if your sling bag's strap is too long, for instance. You can find washboards of all sizes at country music supply web sites, where they are sold as musical instruments.

Speed bump method

I give the credit for this method to John Steinbeck, who took a road trip in the 1960's with his dog and wrote about it in *Travels with Charley*. He managed his laundry rather cleverly by filling a bucket with soapy water and soiled clothing, sealing it, and hanging it off the back of his old rattletrap truck as he bumped and bounced along back country roads. By evening every bit of soil had been agitated out of his clothing. The modern equivalent of this would be to put your knitting in a five-gallon white plastic bucket with a press-seal top, add hot soapy water, and prop it upright securely in the trunk of your car. Then go find some speed bumps to drive over again and again until your knitting is suitably felted. Alternatively, attach two balanced buckets to the panniers of a mountain bike and go for a bumpy trail ride! Knitting can be good exercise.

Using a dryer for special effects

I suspect that in several years, felting in the dryer will have become a fully explored art, but at this time it is in its infancy. So I will share with you what I have discovered, and encourage you to explore further. For best results, I recommend you use the dryer felting method to finish off a piece you have first felted by traditional water immersion methods. At any rate, you must first wash out any excess dye before felting a piece in the dryer, or the dye may adhere to your dryer's drum.

In order for the dryer's tossing and turning to produce felting, the fibers must be thoroughly damp (not dripping wet), so they are soft and open enough to cling to one another. Add a half-dozen tennis balls (for agitation) to your dryer along with the knitting, and set the temperature on warm, remoistening the piece as necessary. The felting will go slowly, taking as long as an hour for something that would take ten minutes in the washing machine, but you have the advantage of being able to examine the piece very easily. You are unlikely to achieve really thick, firm felt this way, but every yarn is different, so experiment.

Here you can see the difference in size and texture before felting (lower photo) and after machine felting (upper photo). The finished piece has transformed from limp and flat to three-dimensional, like woolen pottery.

Substituting yarns and swatching

If you substitute for the yarns called for, you may have somewhat different results. Occasionally even the same yarn in another dye color may felt slightly differently, and the softness or hardness of your water, the kind of soap, and many other variables also affect the final outcome. To use two very different yarns, always check first by knitting a swatch with three inches of one yarn and three of the second. If they felt evenly, you may use them together to produce an even fabric.

When substituting for a yarn in a pattern, choose a feltable yarn (see page 17) of similar yarn wraps per inch (abbreviated as *wpi* - see page 112 for full explanation). If the finished size is important, make a felted test swatch. To swatch, knit and record the measurements of an approximately eight inch square piece, then felt it. After felting, measure again (it may no longer be square). Divide each smaller (felted) measurement by its larger (unfelted) counterpart. The two numbers to the right of the decimal point represent the percentage that the felted piece is of the original length or width. Now calculate the percentage difference between the unfelted and felted measurements of the project you have chosen, see if you are on the right track, and adjust your needle size if needed.

Felted Needle Cozies
A pattern for first time felters

Fine straight knitting needles deserve the shelter of a felted yarn cozy, where they are not only protected and kept together, but may be displayed in groups on a small table, or even arranged as a bouquet in a vase. These small gems take minimal time and yarn, and are a perfect gift for any knitter you know. For your non-knitting friends, they make great cases for an elegant pen or beautiful chopsticks. If you have a collection of leftover colorful balls of yarn tucked away, this may be their happy destiny. If the labels are missing, check for feltability by unspinning a two-inch snippet of yarn, dampening it, and rubbing the fibers firmly and vigorously between the palms of your hands. If it is feltable, the fibers will mat into a little worm of felt in less than a minute.

Yarn: Odds and ends of feltable yarn (see above). Figure on 10 to 20 yards of yarn per cozy. You may knit with two strands of yarn held together, for a cozier cozy.

Needles: You may use any needles that will give you a gauge looser than you would use for a sweater. Depending on the method you choose, you can use double pointed needles, two circular needles, or straight needles.

Notions: Tapestry needle, wooden spoon

Gauge: Approximately 10 - 12 sts = 4" (10 cm)

I suggest that rather than knitting a gauge swatch, then unraveling it and knitting a cozy, just make a cozy and see what happens.

Finished sizes: Small, (medium, large): to fit a pair of *small* needles between sizes 0 - 5 (2 - 3.75 mm), *medium* needles between sizes 6 - 10.5 (4 - 7 mm), or *large* needles between size 11 - 15 (8 - 10 mm). After felting, your needle cozy will be about 80% of its original length and width, and don't forget - you can stop the felting process whenever the cozy seems cozy enough.

Stitch guide: Refer to page 112 for abbreviations.

Felting Guide

Review general felting instructions on pages 16-19. Because you are felting such a narrow tube, it will want to felt itself closed. Just interrupt the washing cycle every minute or two, and stuff the handle of a wooden spoon or spatula inside to free up any clinging fibers. Don't get distracted and forget, or you will have a closed cozy, not what you're after.

Fitting a cozy to your needles

Each of the four methods below will make a cozy to fit small, medium, or large needles (see "finished sizes" on previous page). When a number is followed by two additional numbers in parentheses, these represent the numbers to use for medium and large needles. To make a cozy for a set of double-pointed needles, match the width of the set to the width of a pair of small, medium, or large needles, and follow that size. Make the cozy about 2" taller than the double-pointed needles.

METHOD ONE — TOP DOWN

For a cozy of a single color, or one with stripes that circle, this cozy can be knitted with any style needle.

Cast on 16 (20, 26) sts. Knit and purl alternate rows until cozy measures 9.5" for 7" needles, 12.5" for 10" needles and 17" for 14" needles. For stripes, just change colors whenever you feel like it. On next row, k2tog all the way across (8, 10, 13 sts remain). Cut a 24" tail of yarn and thread the yarn through the stitches, pulling tight and weaving through nearby stitches to secure it. Now use the tail to sew up the side seam. Felt according to instructions on pages 16 - 20.

METHOD TWO — SIDE TO SIDE

For a cozy of a single color, or one with vertical stripes, this cozy can be knitted with any style needle.

For a 10" needle, loosely cast on 40 sts, for a 14" needle, 55 sts. Knit and purl alternate rows until cozy measures 3" (4", 5") from beginning. For stripes, alternate colors every few rows. The cozy to the right is a repeat of two rows purple, 1 row yellow. Loosely cast off. Sew side seam. Close the bottom by sewing through all the edge sts and pulling them tight, sewing securely, and weaving the yarn end inside. Felt according to instructions on pages 16 - 20.

Keeping needle tips cozy

To keep the needle points from poking through the end of the cozy, pad the end with leftover feltable yarn ends before felting. Push them down to the bottom of the cozy with the handle of a wooden spoon, and then sew them lightly in place so they won't drift out during the felting process. They'll thicken and become an impenetrable barrier to protect your fine needles.

METHOD THREE – SPIRALS

These are the best. Once you begin making spiral cozies, you may find it hard to go back to any other kind, because the transformation of the cozy as it becomes a spiral and reveals its full beauty is so thrilling. The knitting is simple, as you will see. This method can be knit with any style needle, and you won't be able to knit just one! Soon your entire stable of loyal knitting needles will be properly clothed and protected. Try arranging a colorful bouquet of needle cozies in a beautiful glass vase. They truly look like a new and marvelous species of flower.

To fit a 10" needle, loosely cast on 45 sts; for a 14" needle, 60 sts. Knit and purl alternate rows, working 2 rows of one color and 3 rows of the main color 3 (4, 5) times. Loosely cast off. Sew side seam. Close the bottom by sewing through all edge sts and pulling until tight, then sewing securely. Felt according to instructions on pages 16 - 20. After felting comes the excitement: Push the cozy onto a spoon handle (or anything of the right size), grip each end of the cozy and twist in opposite directions until you have a spiral. The wooden handle should have just enough friction to keep it in place until the felt dries and is set in spiral form. If not, hunt up some rubber bands and use them to hold it in place until dry. Now make another one!

Try experimenting with thick and thin stripes, irregular stripes, multi-colored yarns, or yarns that felt at drastically different rates. These variations will result in beauty and texture, and you'll experience the awe of witnessing the transformation of unfelted "ugly ducklings" into felted spiral "swans." By the way, nearly everyone twists their spirals in the same direction (see mine?), like it's genetically programmed. Try going the other way sometime!

METHOD FOUR – SEAMLESS

If you like to knit in the round with two circular needles (or double-pointed needles) this method can be used to create a single color cozy or one ringed with stripes. See page 109 for how to knit in the round with two circular needles.

Cast on 12 (16, 20) sts, join (being careful not to twist the line of stitches), and knit until cozy measures 9.5" (for 7" nee-dles), 12.5" (for 10" needles) or 17" (for 14" needles) in length. Knit 2tog all the way around (6, 8, 10 sts remain). Cut a tail of yarn and use the tapestry needle to thread the yarn through the stitches, pulling tight and weaving through nearby stitches to secure it. Felt according to instructions on pages 16 - 20.

Felted Wallets
A pattern for first time felters

Here's a great first project for new knitters as well as seasoned knitters who haven't tried felting yet. You can make the wallets in any size, and leave them plain or embellish them with swirls, or two-color designs. If, like me, you end up knitting yourself a wardrobe of sling bags, you can have a wardrobe of wallets to match! I offer two methods of knitting the wallets, the first in rows, and the second in the round.

Yarn: Each wallet uses about 1 oz of feltable yarn. Check for feltability by unspinning a two-inch snippet of yarn, dampening it, and rubbing the fibers firmly and vigorously between the palms of your hands. If it is feltable, the fibers will mat into a little worm of felt in less than a minute.

Needles: For method one, size 11 (8 mm) needles, straight or circular. For method two, a pair of size 11 (8 mm) circulars, in any lengths *(when knitting with two circular needles, you may use two different lengths, with no problem at all).*

Notions: tapestry needle, matching zipper of any length, since you will cut it to fit; sewing thread to match zipper

Gauge: 12 sts = 4" (10 cm)

Finished size: Before felting, 7" wide and 7.5" deep. After felting, 5.5" wide and 4.75" deep.

Stitch Guide: See page 112 for abbreviations.

Wallet - method one

This method is knit back and forth in rows, then seamed before felting. A zipper is sewn in after felting.

Cast on 24 sts. *Knit 1 row. Purl 1 row. Repeat from * until work measures 6.5", ending with a completed purl row. *Knit 1, ssk, k to 3 sts before end, k2tog, k1. Purl 1, p2tog, p until 3 sts before end, p2tog, p1. Repeat from * once. (16 sts) *Knit 1, k1f&b, k to 2 sts before end, k1f&b, k1. Purl 1, p1f&b, p until 2 sts before end, p1f&b, p1. Repeat from * once. (24 sts) *Knit 1 row. Purl 1 row. Repeat from * until you can fold the piece in half at its narrowest point and the tops match in length. Bind off. Sew sides together. Weave in any ends. Before felting, please review pages 16-19. When the wallet is dry, sew the zipper in with thread, pinning it first so that the sides match. You will find that your stitches sink into the felt and disappear. Tack the ends together where they meet the corners of the wallet, and cut off excess length.

WALLET - METHOD TWO

If you try this method, you will learn one of my favorite tricks - invisibly casting onto two circular needles at once so you can knit a closed tube from the bottom up. If you are a sock-knitter, this method can also be used to begin a toe-up sock.

Use the MCO method to cast on 16 sts, with this change: instead of using the needle and cable of the same needle, use one needle, plus the cable of a second, separate circular needle. You should have 16 sts on each needle, for a total of 32. Now k 1 round using the two circular needle method (see page 109). One needle will have the sts mounted alternately right and wrong, just like the first half of the MCO, so be sure to knit them as they present themselves. After the first round, begin increasing near the ends of each needle: *Knit 1, k1f&b, k until 2 sts remain on needle, k1f&b, k1, repeat from * on second needle. (36 sts) Repeat this round twice. (44 sts) Knit until wallet is 7.5" high. Bind off. Follow felting and zipper instructions for first method.

Choose your own size

Notice that in both methods you are knitting straight except for the base, where there is some shaping. To make the wallet wider or narrower, simply add or subtract stitches at the cast-on. Work the increases or decreases as indicated. If you'd like the wallet to be taller or shorter, just knit more or fewer rows or rounds.

Felting your wallet

Perhaps you are wondering already if the inside of the wallet will fuse shut while felting. It won't! As water rushes back and forth through the wallet, it will push the sides apart as often as it pushes them together. If you are felting your wallet simultaneously with your sling bag, you may want to take the wallet out early, since it doesn't need to felt as firmly as the bag.

EMBELLISHMENTS

Both swirl methods give similar results.
Choose between I-cord or a stockinette roll,
both sewn along a basted path.

Applied I-cord Swirls

Use a needle and contrasting color thread to baste
the path of a swirl (or any design) on an unfelted
knitted piece. Now knit a long rope of I-cord and
sew it on loosely. To knit an I-cord rope, cast on
3 stitches, *knit 3, replace all 3 stitches on left
needle, and repeat from * until you have a long
enough rope. Do not bind off the end of the
I-cord rope until you are finished attaching it, so
that you can knit more or unravel until the length
is just right.

Rolled stockinette swirls

You'll be casting on a lot
of stitches and knitting
about half an inch of
stockinette, then
binding off. Mark
the path of your
design with thread
as described above,
then measure its length. Or just estimate the
length you'll need, knit the roll, and simply sew it
on, making up the design as you go. To knit the
roll, multiply your gauge-per-inch by the desired
length and cast on that number of stitches. Knit
half an inch of stockinette. Bind off. Sew the roll
loosely onto the unfelted knitted piece.

Two-color designs

This wallet has
several inches of a
"knit 1 stitch brown,
knit 1 stitch yellow"
pattern. The brown
bottom intertwines with
the yellow top. Make sure you work two-color
sections loosely, or they will felt more tightly
than the rest of the wallet. If you've never worked
two-color knitting, this is a good small project to
experiment with.

Other possibilities

If you are a needle-felter, you may apply yarn or
fiber designs either before or after felting. If you
apply them before, do so loosely so there is room
for the fiber to shrink at the same rate as the knitted fabric.

An non-felting eyelash yarn can be knit in with
your felting yarn to produce a boa-like effect
around the top of a cozy, the I-cord edge of a
sling bag, or perhaps in the rim of a Fringed
Moebius Bowl or Trifold Bowl. Simply combine
the two yarns wherever you want the furry look,
and you shall have it.

You might like to knit an extra rectangle the size
of the wallet, felt it and sew it inside as a pocket
for credit cards or folded bills. And of course, you
can make the wallet larger so it can hold more, or
knit a flap to fold over and close with a button.

Chapter Two - Magical Baskets

I'd been happily designing and knitting every variation of Moebius scarf I could imagine when one day it popped into my head that it would be possible to "push" a pocket or bowl shape through the scarf's surface. In fact, topologists, the specialized mathematicians who revel in the mystery of the Moebius, playfully call this elastic branch of math "rubber sheet geometry." If they knew how to knit, perhaps they would have named it "knitter's paradise geometry."

STEPS FOR MAKING A MOEBIUS BASKET

- Begin a Moebius band.

- Insert a line of waste yarn stitches before the end of the first round.

- Knit and purl a few rounds, then finish the band off with applied I-cord.

- Pick up the waste yarn stitches and use them to knit the basket's bowl.

Imagine you are a child in a wonderful amusement park which has a huge rubber-sheet Moebius band suspended a few feet above the ground for you to play on. You try to run up the springy, stretchy band as if it were a giant hamster wheel. Your feet push foot shapes through the rubber, and when you lie down, you press a body shape into the elastic material. But no matter what you do, the material is strong enough to keep you from making a hole. Even if a dozen children are playing on the Moebius Band, pressing their feet and noses and legs and bottoms into the rubber material, it continues to have just one surface, one edge, and the single passageway through the center. This is what mathematicians call "rubber sheet geometry," and what we will be knitting.

The Magical Baskets are the simplest of the "rubber sheet" projects. They knit up quickly, take only one skein of yarn, are fun to felt, and make an enchanting gift for just about anyone, even billionaires, who may not own anything quite so intriguing and transformational. As you can see in the photo of my stairs to the left, I have a large collection. I just couldn't stop making one more.

I added a swirl to this basket to help curious people understand that the surface of a Moebius basket is continuous. I ask them to notice how the white swirl travels up the 'outside' surface of the handle and falls down the 'inside' of the bowl, and that to leave the 'inside' of the bowl, they must climb back up the same surface that brought them there, which promptly brings them back 'outside.'

If you've knit a Moebius Scarf, you're already familiar with the first part of the process of knitting a Moebius Basket. After the "scarf" (which becomes handle and rim) is complete, the bowl of the basket is easy to begin. A little waste yarn which was knit into the scarf is removed, and voilà! A temporary slit pops open, lined with stitches just waiting to be knit up, and your Moebius breathes a sigh of relief as it returns to its natural state of Oneness.

FELTED MOEBIUS BASKET

This one-skein basket captivates all who come upon it. At shows I've watched people slowly rotate one in their hands, with the sense of holding something strangely familiar and sacred. "It looks almost like it's made of clay," commented a potter. "It gives me shivers! I'm holding something spiritual," said a storyteller. A naturalist murmured, "They have a domicile effect - as if a creature would like to live inside them." I fill my baskets with flowers, balls of yarn, and acorns, but I love them best empty, so everyone can see and feel the way they welcome you to the radiant dwelling place within.

Yarn: Manos del Uruguay (100% wool, 100 g/ 138 m, 8.5 wpi) 1 skein; 1 yard waste yarn

Needles: (you may require a different size to get correct gauge) size 11 (8 mm) circular, 47" - 55" length, also 16" length

Notions: tapestry needle, stitch markers

Gauge: (before felting) 12 sts = 4" (10 cm)

Finished Size: Before felting: handle 2" x 11.5", rim 22" around, belly 26" around, height 10" from rim to center base. After felting, handle 1.25" x 7.5", rim 16", belly 21", height 6.5".

Stitch Guide: See page 112 for abbreviations, page 110 - 111 for applied I-cord, page 109 for waste yarn and knitting with two circular needles.

Begin handle and rim

With longer needle, MCO 56. Place marker. Knit 84. Use waste yarn to knit next 28 sts. Slide the 28 waste yarn sts back onto left needle. Now knit back across the 28 waste yarn sts on left needle, using regular yarn. Purl 1 round. Knit 1 round.

Finish edge with applied I-cord

Work applied I-cord along entire edge, then graft or sew ends together. You have now completed the handle as well as the rim of the basket.

Bowl of basket

Use 16" circular needle to pick up (but not knit) the 56 sts held by waste yarn. Remove waste yarn. Beginning at one corner, with regular yarn, place marker, *k28, pick up and k 1 extra st in second corner, repeat from * once. (58 sts) *You will need to switch to using both circular needles near the bottom of the basket as they will not all fit on the 16".* It doesn't matter if the two needles are different in length, as long as they are the same size. *Knit 2, k1f&b, repeat from *, end k1.(77 sts) *Knit 24, k1f&b, repeat from * twice, k2. (80 sts) Knit 12 rounds. *Knit 6, k2tog, repeat from * to marker. (70 sts) Knit 4 rounds. *Knit 5, k2tog, repeat from * to marker. (60 sts) Knit 4 rounds. *Knit 4, k2tog, repeat from * to marker. (50 sts) Knit 4 rounds. *Knit 3, k2tog, repeat from * to marker. (40 sts) Knit 1 round.

*Knit 3, k2tog, repeat from * to marker. (32 sts) Knit 1 round. *Knit 2, k2tog, repeat from * to marker. (24 sts) Knit 1 round. *Knit 1, k2tog, repeat from * to marker. (16 sts)

Finishing

Cut tail of yarn. Use tapestry needle to thread tail through all 16 sts and pull tightly closed, weaving end securely. Weave in all ends, and if there are any weak spots in the knitting, especially around the handles, weave extra yarn through these areas to strengthen them before felting.

Felting

Felt according to general instructions on pages 16-19. When felting is complete, pull, push, and pat basket into desired shape, making sure to give the handle a good stretch and then finger-press it smooth. Blowing up a balloon inside the basket and leaving it in place until dry is a reliable way to achieve a round shape.

Yarn and Design Suggestions

Any good felting yarn will work, as long as it felts to a sturdy fabric. Manos of Uruguay is especially wonderful because of its drifting colors, which give the baskets a very organic look. You might sew beads into the knitting before felting, so they will become partly embedded in the felted fibers, appearing as if they are growing there.

SWIRLING MOEBIUS BASKET

The swirl demonstrates to skeptics that indeed, this artful basket has only one surface. Just ask them to follow the yellow line as it coils up and over the handle and drops inside without ever crossing an edge.

Follow directions for Felted Moebius Basket, but purchase 10-20 yards of a contrasting color yarn for the swirl. Refer to page 25 for how to make and add the swirl, which you do before felting.

MOSSY MOEBIUS BASKET

This mossy basket appears to have been lifted from the floor of a lush forest, as if it grew there. When I've given talks or workshops and brought along a collection of Moebius baskets, this is the one people reach for first, because it appears so very alive. You will see quite a transformation between the unfelted fabric and the final result. There is a matching feline bliss bed in Chapter Eight, in case your cat tries to make off with your Mossy Moebius Basket.

Materials: Crystal Palace Labrador (100% thick and thin spun wool, 100 g/ 90 yds, 7.5 wpi), green multi, 3 balls; Crystal Palace Fizz (50 g/ 120 yds, 15 wpi) grass green, 2 balls; 1 yard waste yarn.

Needles: (you may require a different size to get correct gauge) size 11 (8 mm) circular, 47" - 60" length, also 16" length

Notions: tapestry needle, stitch markers

Gauge: (before felting) 12 sts = 4" (10 cm) using one strand of Labrador held together with one strand of Fizz.

Size: Before felting: handle 2" wide, 13" long; rim 30" around, belly 34" around, height 13" from rim to center base. After felting, handle 1.25" wide, 7.5" long, rim 16"; belly 21", height 6.5".

Stitch Guide: See page 112 for abbreviations, page 110 - 111 for applied I-cord, page 109 for waste yarn and knitting with two circular needles.

Knit with both strands of yarn held together throughout.

Begin handle and rim

With longer needle, MCO 70, using one strand of each yarn held together. Place marker. Knit 105. Use waste yarn to knit next 35 sts. Slide the 35 waste yarn sts back onto left needle. Now knit back across the 35 waste yarn sts on left needle using regular yarn. Purl 1 round, k 1 round, p 1 round.

Finish edge with applied I-cord

Work applied I-cord along entire edge, then graft or sew ends together. You have now completed the handle as well as the rim of the basket.

Bowl of basket

Use 16" circular needle to pick up (but not knit) the 70 sts held by waste yarn. Remove waste yarn. Beginning at one corner, with regular yarn, place marker, *k35, pick up and k 1 extra st in second corner, repeat from * once. (72 sts) *You will need to switch to using both circular needles near the bottom of the basket as they will not all fit on the 16".* *Knit 2, k1f&b, repeat from * to marker. (96 sts) *Knit 23, k1f&b, repeat from * to marker. (100 sts) Knit 17 rounds. *Knit 8, k2tog, repeat from * to marker. (90 sts) Knit 4 rounds. *Knit 7, k2tog, repeat from * to marker. (80 sts) Knit 4 rounds. *Knit 6, k2tog, repeat from * to marker. (70 sts) Knit 4 rounds. *Knit 5, k2tog, repeat from * to marker. (60 sts) Knit 2 rounds. *Knit 4, k2tog, repeat from * to marker. (50 sts) Knit 2 rounds. *Knit 3, k2tog, repeat from * to marker. (40 sts) Knit 1 round. *Knit 3, k2tog, repeat from * to marker. (32 sts) Knit 1 round. *Knit 2, k2tog, repeat from * to marker. (24 sts) Knit 1 round. *Knit 1, k2tog, repeat from * to marker. (16 sts) Knit 1 round. *Knit 2 tog, repeat from * to marker. (8 sts)

Finishing

Cut tail of yarn. Use tapestry needle to thread tail through all 16 sts and pull tightly closed, weaving end securely. Weave in all ends, and if there are any weak spots in the knitting, especially around the handles, weave extra yarn through these areas to strengthen them before felting.

Felting

Felt according to general instructions on pages 16-19. When felting is complete, pull, push, and pat basket into desired shape, making sure to give the handle a good stretch and then finger-press it smooth. Do not use a balloon to give the basket shape as it will matt the moss. This basket is meant to be bumpy and beautiful, like nature.

Yarn and design suggestions

If you want your Mossy Moebius Basket to look like this one, you'll need to use the same yarns, or something similar. The wool yarn sinks beneath the feathery strands of eyelash yarn, yet reveals its mossy blur of yellows and greens. Look for a thick and thin worsted or bulky weight yarn and a complimentary eyelash, and remember that moss can grow in slate and autumn colors as well. You may also use this pattern with one strand of a felting yarn to make a Moebius basket that is larger than the first one in this chapter.

SHAPE DU JOUR MOEBIUS BASKETS

These baskets, although knit of a yarn with no elasticity (Deco-Ribbon), turns out to be surprisingly elastic and will accept bowls of many shapes, hugging them to make a lovely planter, nut bowl, or bread basket. This allows you to not only reshape the basket at whim, but also to add water and flowers or small plants. The two baskets you see are identical in size, but the brown one is embracing a ball-shaped bowl and the green one takes the shape of a low, wide bowl.

Materials: Crystal Palace Deco-Ribbon (70% acrylic, 30% nylon, 50 g/ 80 yds, wpi is too difficult to measure because this is a ribbon yarn), 2 balls, 1 yd waste yarn.

Needles: (you may require a different size to get correct gauge) size 9 (5.5 mm) circular, 40" length, also 16" circular
Notions: tapestry needle, stitch markers
Gauge: 4 sts = 1" (10 cm)
Finished size: handle 1.5" x 8.5", rim 14" circumference, belly 17" circumference, height 5.5" from rim to center base.
Stitch Guide: See page 112 for abbreviations, page 110 - 111 for applied I-cord, page 109 for waste yarn and knitting with two circular needles.

Begin handle and rim

With longer needle, MCO 56. Place marker. *Knit 1, p1, repeat from * 27 times (now marker is *on cable below needles*). Use waste yarn to k next 22 sts. Slide the 22 waste yarn sts back onto left needle. Knit 1, p1 back across the 22 waste yarn sts on left needle, using regular yarn. Continue k1, p1 pattern to marker. *Purl 1, k1, repeat from * to marker. *Knit 1, p1, repeat from * to marker. *Purl 1, k1, repeat from * to marker.

Finish edge with applied I-cord

Work applied I-cord along entire edge, then graft or sew ends together. You have completed the handle as well as the rim of the basket.

Bowl of basket

Use 16" needle to pick up (but not knit) the 22 sts held by the waste yarn. Use 40" needle to pick up second 22 sts. Remove waste yarn. Working with both circular needles, *place marker, and with regular yarn k22, pick up and knit 2 extra in corner, repeat from * once. (48 sts) *Knit 1, k1f&b, repeat from *. (72 sts) Knit 14 rounds. After a few rounds you will be able to fit all the sts on the 16" needle. Place a marker at the beginning (near the yarn attachment) if you change to one needle. *You will need to work with two circular needles once you begin to decrease after completing the 14 rounds.* *Knit 2, k2tog, k3, k2tog, repeat from * to marker. (56 sts) Knit 3 rounds. *Knit 3, k2tog, repeat from * to marker, end k1. (45 sts) Knit 2 rounds. *Knit 3, k2tog, repeat from * to marker. (36 sts) Knit 2 rounds. *Knit 4, k2tog, repeat from * to marker. (30 sts) Knit 1 round. *Knit 3, k2tog, repeat from * to marker. (24 sts) Knit 1 round. *Knit 2, k2tog, repeat from * to marker. (18 sts) Knit 1 round. *Knit 1, k2tog, repeat from * to marker. (12 sts) Knit 1 round. *Knit 2 tog, repeat from * to marker. (6 sts)

Finishing

Cut tail of yarn. Use tapestry needle to thread tail through all 6 sts and pull tightly closed, weaving end securely. Weave in any other ends. The basket does not require any blocking, since you will be inserting small bowls of various shapes and sizes inside and it will wrap itself snug around them.

I don't know if I wear the bag or the bag wears me! It conforms to the body so beautifully and sensually. It's an ergonomic, intelligent bag.
Magical Knitting Workshop student, Vancouver, B.C.

CHAPTER THREE - FELTED SLING BAGS

My first Moebius sling bag emerged from a failed scarf design. For months I'd entertained visions of an elegant Moebius scarf with three long, pennant-like triangles growing from it, one trailing down the back and the other two flowing from each side. These "tails" could be looped together, or thrown over the back. In my mind's eye, it seemed stunning.

One night I began knitting the scarf in a dreamy white alpaca, finished the first long triangle, and eagerly tried it on, with the triangle trailing down my back. To my disappointment, it looked just plain silly. So I began fiddling with it in front of the mirror, rotating the triangle around, and when it fell to my side, it suddenly became a mysterious sling bag! (This sort of surprise-via-failure, by the way, is how many designs arrive, detouring right around my brain.) The bag's long, narrow shape was beautiful but impractical. So I unraveled the triangle nearly to the scarf (which was now to serve as a strap, not a scarf), and knit the shape you see here. Then I threw the whole thing in the washer to felt it down to size. By now it was midnight.

At one in the morning, I stood wearily in front of the mirror again, wearing the damp sling bag, awed by its beauty. The strap resting on my shoulder felt like a warm, trusted hand, while the bag nestled against my side like a drowsy baby. I fell happily into bed and in the morning began designing more bags with a passion.

You may wonder about the twisted strap, and I did too, until I tried it on, and discovered that the twist is a good thing. It tips the bag into your waist and funnels down into the opening, like a pathway carved by a waterfall. The wide strap is designed to be worn *right on your shoulder*, not pressing against your neck. You can't imagine how good that "warm hand" strap feels. I often come home and leave my bag on for a while as I putter around the house.

Right-and left-sided versions

The bag is designed to be worn as shown, with the half-twist lying in front. For a right hip version, make sure the needle lies on *top* of the cable when you check for one crossing of needle and cable. For the left hip version, make sure the needle lies *under* the cable. See page twelve for clear instructions.

Customizing strap length

You'll find directions in each pattern to adjust the strap length to fit the intended wearer. Long pieces of knitting, such as a strap, do not felt at the same rate as more compact shapes, like the bag itself, and I have worked out the formulas for each pattern. If after felting and drying, the strap is still too long, wrap the strap (not the bag) in a wet towel for an hour. Then wrap a dry towel around the bag only, secure the towel with safety pins, and throw the protected bag with its unprotected damp strap in a hot dryer with a half dozen tennis balls. Check it every five minutes while the strap slowly felts a little more. And if the strap is too short, just wear it for a day or two, as it will probably stretch out a little.

Wallets

Wallets to go with the sling bags can be found in Chapter One, along with instructions for adding embellishments.

Moebius Sling Bag, Winter weight

The winter weight bags are knit with a double strand of yarn, allowing the purl ridges to rise and catch the light as a simple yet elegant design element. If you've knit Moebius scarves from the first Treasury, you may notice that the bag's strap and rim are actually a Purl Ridge Moebius Scarf with a waste yarn opening for knitting the bag. The knitting is easy, and the results so comforting to wear that you may find yourself making a colorful collection of these cozy bags.

Directions below include both the teal bag shown on this page, and the yellow version with brown trim shown on the previous page.

Yarn: Cascade 220 (100% wool, 100 g/ 220 yds, 13 wpi). Teal version: teal, 3 skeins. Yellow version: Cascade 220 Tweed (100% wool, 100 g/ 220 yds, 13 wpi), yellow, 2 skeins, brown, 1 skein; 1 yd waste yarn.

Needles: (you may require a different size to get correct gauge) size 11 (8 mm) circular, 47" - 60" length, also 16" length

Notions: tapestry needle, stitch markers

Gauge: (before felting) 12 sts = 4" (10 cm) with 2 strands of yarn held together

Finished size: Before felting, bag is 14" deep, 12.5" wide; strap 54" long, 6" wide. After felting, bag is 11" deep, 10.5" wide; strap 48" long, 5" wide.

Fitting guide: Loop tape measure around yourself, over one shoulder and falling at the opposite hip. Multiply this measurement by 3.3. This is your personal MCO number (round off to a whole number), and together with correct gauge, will give you a custom fit. Pattern as written is for a 48" strap (average woman).

Stitch Guide: See page 112 for abbreviations, page 110 - 111 for applied I-cord, page 109 for waste yarn and knitting with two circular needles. *Work with double strand of yarn throughout.*

Begin Moebius strap and rim of bag

With double strand of yarn, MCO 160 (or personal MCO number, see fitting guide). Place marker. Knit 160 (or personal MCO), k 35 with waste yarn, replace waste yarn loops on left needle. With regular yarn, k into each waste yarn loop, then continue knitting to marker. Knit 2 rounds. *Purl 3 rounds, k 3 rounds, repeat from *once.

Applied I-cord edge

Work applied I-cord until all sts are bound off, using double strand of brown yarn if making yellow bag. Graft or sew I-cord ends together.

Begin bag

Place the 70 waste yarn sts on 16" needle, picking up 2 extra sts at each corner. (74 sts) Remove waste yarn. Place markers in center of each corner. (37 sts between markers) *Knit 2 rounds. *Knit 1, ssk, k to within 3 sts of next marker, k2tog, k1, repeat from * once. (70 sts) Purl 2 rounds. *Purl 1, p2tog, p to within 3 sts of next marker, p2tog, p1, repeat from * once. (66 sts) Repeat last 6 rounds once. (58 sts)

Bag widens & grows downward

*Knit 2, k1f&b, repeat until 4 sts remain before second marker, end k4. (76 sts) Knit for 5".

Bag narrows & closes

You will need to switch to using both circular needles near the bottom of the bag as they will not all fit on the 16". *Knit 1, ssk, k to within 3 sts of next marker, k2tog, k1, repeat from * once. Knit 1 round. Repeat last 2 rounds 4 times. (56 sts) Now work decrease round every round until 32 sts remain. Close bottom with a 3-needle bind-off, or bind off and sew together. Weave in all ends.

Felting and finishing

Felt according to general instructions on pages 16-19. Felt, checking every few minutes until strap is an inch or so shorter than desired length. Spin dry, then block as follows: put on bag, and with strap resting on shoulder edge, place other hand into bag and press down hard (strap will grow about an inch). Now either blow a balloon up in the bag or shape it by hand. Let dry and enjoy!

Yarn and design suggestions

If substituting another feltable yarn, see page 19 for swatch instructions. You can add any of the embellishments described on page 25, or sew on beads. If you add the beads before felting, they will slightly embed in the felt and resemble seeds planted in colorful soil.

Moebius Sling Bag, summer weight

I made my first Moebius Sling Bags in winter, when woolly warmth was wanted. But as the tulips began to blossom, I switched to this lighter version, knit with one strand of wool instead of two. You may knit yours all in one color, or with stripes as shown. I've worn these bags even while teaching in a California summer heat wave, and surprisingly, still found it comfortable. Wool breathes!

Yarn: Cascade 220 (100% wool, 100 g/ 220 yds, 13 wpi), brown, 2 skeins; green, 1 skein; for a single color bag, 2 skeins; 1 yd waste yarn

Needles: (you may require a different size to get correct gauge) size 11 (8 mm) circular, 47" - 60" length, also 16" length

Notions: tapestry needle, stitch markers

Gauge: (before felting) 12 sts = 4" (10 cm)

Finished size: Before felting, bag is 14" deep, 12.5" wide; strap 54" long, 6" wide. After felting, bag is 11" deep, 10.5" wide; strap 48" long, 5" wide.

Fitting guide: Loop a tape measure around yourself, over one shoulder and falling at the opposite hip. Multiply this measurement by 3.3. This is your personal MCO number (round off to a whole number), and together with correct gauge, will give you a custom fit. Pattern as written is for a 48" strap (average woman).

Stitch Guide: See page 112 for abbreviations, page 110 - 111 for applied I-cord, page 109 for waste yarn and knitting with two circular needles.

If making a single color bag, follow directions without cutting or changing yarn.

Begin Moebius strap and rim of bag

With brown, MCO 160 (or personal MCO number, see fitting guide). Place marker. Knit 160 (or personal MCO), k 35 with waste yarn, replace waste yarn loops on left needle. With brown yarn, knit into each waste yarn loop, then all the way to marker. Knit 1 more round, cut tail of brown. *With green, p 3 rounds. Cut tail of green, and with brown, k 3 rounds. Cut tail of brown. Repeat from * once.

Applied I-cord edge

With green, work applied I-cord until all sts are bound off. Graft or sew I-cord ends together.

Begin bag

Place the 70 waste yarn sts on 16" needle, picking up 2 sts at each corner. (74 sts) Remove waste yarn. Place a marker in center of each corner. (37 sts between markers) *If using a single color, skip ahead to next italicized line.* Notice that there are 2 rows of brown on one side and 3 on the other. Beginning on the side with 2 rows, knit side facing you, using brown yarn, knit 37 sts (making 3 rows of brown on each side). Cut tail of brown. *If using a single color, begin here.* With green, k 2 rounds. *Knit 1, ssk, k to within 3 sts of next marker, k2tog, k1, repeat from * once. Repeat last 3 rounds 3 times, changing to brown for first repeat, green for second repeat, then brown for the third repeat and the rest of the bag. (58 sts)

Bag widens & grows downward
*Knit 2, k1f&b, repeat until 4 sts remain before second marker, end k4. (76 sts) Knit for 5".

Bag narrows & closes
You will need to switch to using both circular needles near the bottom of the bag as they will not all fit on the 16". Knit 2 rounds. *Knit 1, ssk, k to within 3 sts of next marker, k2tog, k1, repeat from * once. Knit 1 round. Repeat last 2 rounds 4 times. (56 sts) Now work decrease round every round until 32 sts remain. Close bottom with a 3-needle bind-off, or bind off and sew together. Weave in all ends.

Felting and finishing
Felt according to general instructions on pages 16-19. Felt, checking every few minutes until strap is an inch or so shorter than desired length. Spin dry, then block as follows: put on bag, and with strap resting on shoulder edge, place other hand into bag and press down hard (strap will grow about an inch). Now either blow a balloon up in the bag or shape it by hand. Let dry and enjoy!

Yarn and design suggestions
If substituting another feltable yarn, see page 19 for swatch instructions. You can add any of the embellishments described on page 25, or sew on beads before felting, so they will embed themselves organically. If you'd like a winter weight version, just double the strands of yarn, and the stripes will undulate with thicker ridges.

Persian Bag
with Pouch

The motif on this bag is an ancient design from Persia. You may also make this bag with a doubled strand of yarn for a winter weight version.

Yarn: Cascade 220 (100% wool, 220 yds/ 100 g, 13 wpi), brown and rose, 1 skein each; green, 2 skeins; 1 yd waste yarn

Needles: (you may require a different size to get correct gauge) size 11 (8 mm) circular, 47" to 60" length, also 16" length

Notions: tapestry needle, stitch markers

Gauge: (before felting) 12 sts = 4" (10 cm)

Finished size: Before felting, bag is 13" deep, 12" wide, pouch 7.5" deep, 8.5" wide, strap 54" long, 8" wide. After felting, bag is 10.5" deep, 9" wide, pouch 5.5" deep, 6.5" wide, strap 48" long, 5" wide.

Fitting guide: Loop a tape measure around yourself like the strap of the sling bag, over one shoulder and falling at the opposite hip. Multiply this measurement by 3.3. This is your personal MCO number (round off to a whole number), and together with correct gauge, will give you a custom fit. Pattern as written is for a 48" strap (average woman).

Stitch Guide: See page 112 for abbreviations, page 110 - 111 for applied I-cord, page 109 for waste yarn and knitting with two circular needles.

Begin Moebius strap and rim
With green, MCO 160 (or personal MCO number, see fitting guide). Place marker. Knit 160 (or personal MCO number), k35 with waste yarn, replace waste yarn sts on left needle, and with regular yarn, k into each waste yarn loop, then k to marker. Knit 2 more rounds, cut tail of green. With brown, p 3 rounds, k 3 rounds, cut tail of brown. With green, p 3 rounds, k 3 rounds.

Applied I-cord edge
With brown, work applied I-cord until all sts are bound off. Graft or sew I-cord ends together.

Begin bag and Persian design
Place the 70 waste yarn sts on 16" needle, picking up 2 sts at each corner, then remove waste yarn. (74 sts) Place markers in center of each corner. (37 sts between markers) With green, k 2 rounds. Knit 2tog, k to second marker, k2tog, k to first marker. (72 sts) Knit 1 round. Knit 6, k24 with waste yarn, replace waste yarn loops on left needle, and k over them with green. Knit to first marker. Knit 1 round. Repeat decrease round as above. (70 sts) Begin repeats of Persian design in rose and green. These 10 rows of stranded knitting will pull in slightly, shaping the bag's neck.

Bag widens & grows downward

When design is complete, continue with green only. Knit 1 round. *Knit 6, k1f&b, repeat from * 9 times. (80 sts) Continue until bag measures 11" from rim.

Bag narrows & closes

You will need to switch to using both circular needles near the bottom of the bag as they will not all fit on the 16". Knit 2 rounds. *Knit 1, ssk, k to within 3 sts of next marker, k2tog, k1, repeat from * once. Knit 1 round. Repeat last 2 rounds 4 times. (60 sts) Now work decrease round every round until 44 sts remain. Turn bag inside out, and close with a 3-needle bind-off, or bind off and sew together. Weave in all ends.

Pouch

With 16" needle, pick up the 48 sts held by waste yarn, and pick up 3 sts in each corner. (54 sts) With green, k until pouch is 6" long from beginning round. *Knit 2 rounds. *Knit 1, ssk, k to within 3 sts of next marker, k2tog, k1, repeat from * once. Repeat last round until 30 sts remain. Turn bag inside out. Close with a 3-needle bind-off, or bind off and sew together. Weave in all ends.

Felting and finishing

Felt according to general instructions on pages 16-19. Felt, checking every few minutes until strap is an inch or so shorter than desired length. Spin dry, then block as follows: put on bag, and with strap resting on shoulder edge, place other hand into bag and press down hard (strap will grow about an inch). Now either blow a balloon up in the bag or shape it by hand. Let dry and enjoy!

HOW TO ADD POUCHES ANYWHERE YOU LIKE

You can add a pouch to any sling bag by simply knitting in a line of waste yarn where you want the pouch to be, and when the rest of the bag is finished, pick up the waste yarn stitches to knit the pouch. It is even possible to decide to add a pouch later, without having knit in the waste yarn (as in Elizabeth Zimmermann's "afterthought pockets"). Snip one strand in a row, and it will unravel sideways. Then you can pick up the newly orphaned stitches for your pouch. Of course, all this must be done before felting.

You can add pouches to bags, bowls, baskets, or branch out into tentacles (see Chapter Five), use waste yarn when you suddenly decide you want handles on an unfelted container, add a pocket to a sweater … this is one of those nifty little knitting tricks that you will use forever.

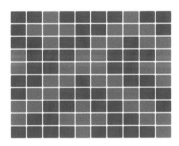

The Persian design is a 10-stitch repeat worked over 11 rounds.

Child's Swirl Sling Bag

During a Magical Knitting Workshop at a local library, I mentioned that I still needed a child to model these bags. A moment later, one of my students spied little Alyssa out in the lobby. I ran out and explained to her grandfather, whose arms were full of picture books, why I'd love to photograph his granddaughter. He was wonderfully cautious, such a good protector, and only after I promised not to use the photos without the parents' permission, did he say yes. He and the angelic two year old Alyssa joined us in the classroom, where she won all our hearts, and has probably won yours now too. Here you see her gazing adoringly at her dear grandfather. Although the bag is a little too long for her, she will grow into it, and we all agreed that she was the perfect model.

Yarn: Cascade 220 (100% wool, 220 yds/ 100 g, 13 wpi), green, brown, and blue, 1 skein each; 1 yd waste yarn

Needles: (you may require a different size to get correct gauge) size 11 (8 mm) circular, 47" length, also 16" length

Notions: tapestry needle, stitch markers

Gauge: (before felting) 12 sts = 4" (10 cm)

Finished size: Before felting, bag is 9.5" deep, 9" wide, strap 40" long, 3.5" wide. After felting, 7" deep, 7" wide, 35" long, 2.5" wide.

Fitting guide: Loop a tape measure around the child, over one shoulder and falling at the opposite hip. Multiply this measurement by 3.6. This is the child's personal MCO number (round off to a whole number), and together with correct gauge, will give a custom fit. Pattern as written is for a 35" strap, suitable for a 3 to 4 year-old.

Stitch Guide: See page 112 for abbreviations, page 110 - 111 for applied I-cord, page 109 for waste yarn and knitting with two circular needles.

Begin Moebius strap and rim of bag

With green yarn, MCO 125 (or personal MCO number, see fitting guide). Place marker. Knit 125, k 30 with waste yarn, replace on left needle, and knit into each waste yarn loop, then knit as usual to marker. Knit 1 round, and cut tail of yarn. *With blue, p 3 rounds. Cut tail of blue. With green, k 3 rounds.

Applied I-cord edge

With brown, work applied I-cord until all sts are bound off. Graft or sew I-cord ends together.

Here's another version, worked in two colors, camel and blue jeans.

Felting and finishing

Felt according to general instructions on pages 16-19. Felt, checking every few minutes until strap is an inch shorter than desired length. Spin dry, then block as follows: hold strap, place other hand into bag and press down hard (strap will grow about an inch). Now either blow a balloon up in the bag or shape it by hand. Let dry, and it's ready for that dear little person.

Begin bag

Place the 60 waste yarn sts on 16" needle, picking up 2 sts at each corner, remove waste yarn. (64 sts) Place markers in center of each corner. (32 sts between markers) With blue, k 2 rounds. Cut tail of blue. With green, k 2 rounds. *Knit 1, ssk, k to within 3 sts of next marker, k2tog, k1, repeat from * once. Knit 1 round. Repeat last 2 rounds 4 times. (44 sts)

Bag widens and grows downward

*Knit 2, k1f&b, repeat from * to first marker, end k2. (58 sts) Knit 1 round. K1f&b after each marker. (60 sts). Knit for 3".

Bag narrows at bottom and closes

Switch to using both circular needles near the bottom of the bag, as they will not all fit on the 16".
*Knit 2 rounds. *Knit 1, ssk, k to within 3 sts of next marker, k2tog, k1, repeat from * once. Repeat last round 4 times. (40 sts) Work decrease round every round until 24 sts remain. Turn bag inside out, and close with a 3-needle bind-off, or bind off and sew together. Weave in all ends.

Swirl

See page 25 for directions. You will need approximately 1 yard of I-cord in contrast color.

DIAMOND SLING BAG

There's just a few inches of two-color knitting involved in these cheerful bags, although if you prefer, you could work the diamonds in duplicate stitch. You may notice that the stripes on the blue bag's strap are thinner than the stripes on the red bag's strap. For the thinner stripes, follow the strap directions for the Moebius Sling Bag, Summer Weight, the second pattern in this chapter.

Yarn: Cascade 220 (100% wool, 100 g/ 220 yds, 13 wpi), main color: garnet or royal blue, 2 skeins; 1 skein contrast color for stripes and diamonds, (optional: 25 yards second contrast color for diamonds); 1 yd waste yarn

Needles: (you may require a different size to get correct gauge) size 11 (8 mm) circular, 47" - 60" length, also 16" length

Notions: tapestry needle, stitch markers

Gauge: (before felting) 12 sts = 4" (10 cm)

Finished size: Before felting, bag is 14" deep, 12.5" wide, strap 54" long, 6" wide. After felting, bag is 11" deep, 10.5" wide, strap 48" long, 5" wide.

Fitting guide: Loop a tape measure around yourself, over one shoulder and falling at the opposite hip. Multiply this measurement by 3.3. This is your personal MCO number (round off to a whole number), and together with correct gauge, will give you a custom fit. Pattern as written is for a 48" strap (average woman).

Stitch Guide: See page 112 for abbreviations, page 110 - 111 for applied I-cord, page 109 for waste yarn and knitting with two circular needles.

Strap

With main color, MCO 160 (or personal MCO number, see fitting guide). Place marker. Knit 160 (or personal MCO number), k35 with waste yarn, replace waste yarn sts on left needle, and with main color, knit into each waste yarn loop, then all the way to marker. Knit 2 more rounds, cut tail of main color. With contrast color, p 3 rounds and k 3 rounds, cut tail of contrast color. With main color, p 3 rounds and k 3 rounds.

Applied I-cord edge

With contrast color, work applied I-cord until all sts are bound off. Graft or sew I-cord ends together.

Begin bag

Place the 70 waste yarn sts on 16" needle, picking up 2 sts at each corner. (74 sts) Remove waste yarn. Place a marker in center of each corner. (37 sts between markers) With main color, k 2 rounds. Knit 2tog, knit to next marker, k2tog. (72 sts) Knit 1 round. Add contrast color and begin 9-st repeats of diamond design starting at first marker. The bag will pull in slightly because of the stranded knitting, and help shape the neck.

Bag widens & grows downward

When diamond design is complete, k 2 rounds. Knit 17, k1f&b. (76 sts) Continue until knitting measures 5" from bottom tips of diamonds to needle.

Bag narrows & closes

You will need to switch to using both circular needles near the bottom of the bag as they will not all fit on the 16". *Knit 1, ssk, k to within 3 sts of next marker, k2tog, k1, repeat from * once. Knit 1 round. Repeat last 2 rounds 4 times. (56 sts) Now work decrease round every round until 32 sts remain. Close bottom with a 3-needle bind-off, or bind off and sew together. Weave in all ends.

Felting and finishing

Felt according to general instructions on pages 16-19. Felt, checking every few minutes until strap is an inch or so shorter than desired length. Spin dry, then block as follows: put on bag, with strap resting on shoulder edge, and place other hand into bag and press down hard (strap will grow about an inch). Now either blow a balloon up in the bag or shape it by hand.
Let dry and enjoy!

Yarn and design suggestions

If substituting another feltable yarn, see page 19 for swatch instructions. You can add any of the embellishments described on page 25, sew on beads, or add a pouch (see Persian Bag pattern in this chapter). If you'd like to make the striped version in a winter weight, just double the strands of yarn, and the stripes will be even more pronounced because of the way the thicker yarn creates ridges of texture.

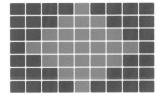

The diamond design is a 9-stitch repeat over 7 rounds.

SPACIOUS SHOW & TELL MOEBIUS BAG

Follow the blue swirl design on this extra large bag, as it dips into the pouch and then meanders out to follow the strap, finally wandering down to the bag's interior. Does it ever leave the surface? No! With this bag you can demonstrate the Moebius mysteries to everyone you meet. Go forth and educate!

Yarn: Lana Grossa Royal Tweed (100% Merino Fine, 50 g/ 100 m, 9 wpi), persimmon, 5 balls; blue, 1 ball; 2 yds waste yarn

Needles: (you may require a different size to get correct gauge) size 11 (8 mm) circular, 47" - 60" length, also 16 - 24" length

Notions: tapestry needle, stitch markers

Gauge: (before felting) 14 sts = 4" (10 cm)

Finished size: Before felting, outer bag is 19" deep and 17" wide. Inner bag is 9" deep and 9" wide. Strap is 56" long and 6" wide. After felting, outer bag is 13" deep and 13" wide, inner bag is 7" deep and 7" wide. Strap is 48" long and 4" wide.

Fitting guide: Loop a tape measure around yourself, over one shoulder and falling at the opposite hip. Multiply this measurement by 3.4. This is your personal MCO number (round off to a whole number) and with correct gauge will give you a custom fit. Pattern as written is for a 48" strap (average woman).

Stitch Guide: See page 112 for abbreviations, page 110 - 111 for applied I-cord, page 109 for waste yarn and knitting with two circular needles.

Begin Moebius strap and rim of bag

With persimmon, MCO 165 (or personal MCO number, see fitting guide). Place marker. Knit 165 (or personal MCO number), k50 with waste yarn, replace waste yarn sts on left needle, and k into each waste yarn loop with regular yarn, then k all the way to marker. Knit 2 rounds. *Purl 3 rounds, k 3 rounds, repeat from * once.

Applied I-cord edge

Work applied I-cord until all sts are bound off. Graft or sew I-cord ends together.

Begin bag

Place the 100 waste yarn sts on shorter needle, picking up 2 sts at each corner, then remove waste yarn. (104 sts) Place markers in center of each corner. (52 sts between markers) Knit 2 rounds. *Knit 1, ssk, k to within 3 sts of next marker, k2tog, k1, repeat from * once. (100 sts) Purl 2 rounds. *Purl 1, p2tog, p to within 3 sts of next marker, p2tog, p1, repeat from * once. (96 sts) Knit 1 round. Knit 12, k 24 with waste yarn, replace waste yarn sts on left needle, k into each waste yarn loop with regular yarn, k to end of round. *Knit 1, ssk, k to within 3 sts of next marker, k2tog, k1, repeat from * once. (92 sts) Purl 2 rounds. *Purl 1, p2tog, p to within 3 sts of next marker, p2tog, p1, repeat from * once. (88 sts) Knit 1 round.

Bag widens & grows downward

Knit 2, k1f&b, repeat from *, end k1, k1f&b, k1, k1f&b. (118 sts) Continue until knitting measures 8" from last purl ridge.

Bag narrows & closes

*Knit 1, ssk, k to within 3 sts of marker, k2tog, k1, repeat from * once. Knit 1 round. Repeat from * 5 times. (94 sts) Now work decrease row every row until 54 sts remain. Turn bag inside out, and close with a 3-needle bind-off, or bind off and sew together. Weave in all ends.

Pouch

With shorter needle, pick up the 48 sts held by waste yarn, and pick up 3 sts in each corner. (54 sts) Knit all rounds until pouch is 8" long from beginning round. *Knit 1, ssk, k to within 3 sts of next marker, k2tog, k1, repeat from * once. (50 sts) Repeat last round twice. (42 sts) Close with a 3-needle bind-off, or bind off and sew together.

Swirl

See page 25 for directions. You will need approximately 2.5 yards of I-cord in Sky. Loosely sew I-cord in swirling design, following path in and out of pouch, up over strap and down into bag's interior.

Felting and finishing

Felt according to general instructions on pages 16-19. During felting process, check every few minutes until strap is an inch or so shorter than desired length. Spin dry, then block as follows: put on bag, and with strap resting on shoulder edge, place other hand into bag and press down hard (strap will grow about an inch). Now either blow a balloon up in the bag or shape it by hand. Let dry and enjoy!

Spacious Desert Sunrise Bag

Here's a strikingly different version of the Spacious Sling Bag, thanks to the hand-dyed yarn. The color design around the belly of this bag is the result of two elements. The first is the yarn itself, a hand-paint with a large section of green followed by shorter sections of the colors you see in between the green sides. The second element is that the bag's belly uses exactly two skein circumferences of yarn each round (if your gauge is accurate!). As you can see, once the bag begins to decrease at the bottom, the patterning changes, because now the colors do not lie on top of one another as they did in the skein. If you wish to substitute with another yarn, look for a hand-painted yarn with a 64" skein circumference, like Wool in the Woods Star City Wool. But no matter what you do, your bag will be unique, because each skein of hand-painted yarn is one-of-a-kind.

Yarn: Wool in the Woods Star City Wool (100% wool, 140 g/ 200 yds, 10 wpi), 3 skeins Desert Sunrise, 1 skein Adobe; 2 yds waste yarn

Needles: (you may require a different size to get correct gauge) size 11 (8 mm) circular, 47" - 60" length, also 16 - 24" length

Notions: tapestry needle, stitch markers

Gauge: (before felting) 14 sts = 4" (10 cm)

Finished size: Before felting, outer bag is 19" deep, 17" wide; inner bag 9" deep, 9" wide, strap 56" long, 6" wide. After felting, outer bag is 13" deep, 13" wide, inner bag 7" deep, 7" wide, strap 48" long, 4" wide.

Fitting guide: Loop a tape measure around yourself, over one shoulder and falling at the opposite hip. Multiply this measurement by 3.4. This is your personal MCO number (round off to a whole number) and with correct gauge will give you a custom fit. Pattern as written is for a 48" strap (average woman).

Stitch Guide: See page 112 for abbreviations, page 110 - 111 for applied I-cord, page 109 for waste yarn and knitting with two circular needles.

Begin Moebius strap and rim

MCO 165 (or personal MCO number, see fitting guide). Place marker. Knit 165 (or personal MCO number), k50 with waste yarn, replace waste yarn sts on left needle, and k into each waste yarn loop with regular yarn, then k all the way to marker. Knit 2 rounds. *Purl 3 rounds, k 3 rounds, repeat from * once.

Applied I-cord edge

With Adobe, work applied I-cord until all sts are bound off. Graft or sew I-cord ends together.

Begin bag

Place the 100 waste yarn sts on shorter needle, picking up 2 sts at each corner, then remove waste yarn. (104 sts) Place markers in center of each corner. (52 sts between markers) Knit 2 rounds. *Knit 1, ssk, k to within 3 sts of next marker, k2tog, k1, repeat from * once. (100 sts) Purl 2 rounds. *Purl 1, p2tog, p to within 3 sts of next marker, p2tog, p1, repeat from * once. (96 sts) Knit 1 round. Knit 12, k 24 with waste yarn, replace waste yarn sts on left needle, k into each waste yarn loop with regular yarn, k to end of round. *Knit 1, ssk, k to within 3 sts of next marker, k2tog, k1, repeat from * once. (92 sts) Purl 2 rounds. *Purl 1, p2tog, p to within 3 sts of next marker, p2tog, p1, repeat from * once. (88 sts) Knit 1 round.

Bag widens & grows downward

Knit 2, k1f&b, repeat from *, end k1, k1f&b, k1, k1f&b. (118 sts) Continue until knitting measures 8" from last purl ridge.

Bag narrows & closes

*Knit 1, ssk, k to within 3 sts of next marker, k2tog, k1, repeat from * once. Knit 1 round. Repeat from * 5 times. (94 sts) Now work decrease row every row until 54 sts remain. Turn bag inside out, and close with a 3-needle bind-off, or bind off and sew together. Weave in all ends.

Pouch

With shorter needle, pick up the 48 sts held by waste yarn, plus 3 sts in each corner. (54 sts) Knit all rounds until pouch is 8" long from beginning round. *Knit 1, ssk, k to within 3 sts of next marker, k2tog, k1, repeat from * once. (50 sts) Repeat last round twice. (42 sts) Close with a 3-needle bind-off, or bind off and sew together.

Felting and finishing

Felt according to general instructions on pages 16-19. Felt, checking every few minutes until strap is an inch or so shorter than desired length. Spin dry, then block as follows: put on bag, and with strap resting on shoulder edge, place other hand into bag and press down hard (strap will grow about an inch). Now either blow a balloon up in the bag or shape it by hand.
Let dry and enjoy!

Llama Lucretia is the shepherdess of a herd of sheep here on San Juan Island.

Magical knitting has reawakened my passion for knitting.
email from reader of the first Treasury

Chapter Four - Unfelted Sling bags

These unfelted bags are ready to go out the door to see the world with you the minute they come off your needles. Knit of plant fibers like cotton, linen, and rayon, they also offer the natural ventilation you want in warmer weather.

If you've read the previous chapter, you'll find that these bags follow the same method, but are knit at a smaller gauge since the unfelted fabric must to be sturdy enough to function as an unlined purse.

If you would like to line these bags, carefully trace the finished bag's shape on a brown paper bag, adding another half inch or so for a seam allowance. Use the pattern to cut out two pieces of your fabric. Place right sides together, and sew the edges, leaving the top unsewn. Iron the top seam allowance towards the wrong side, then hand sew it along the inside of the bag's rim.

Feel free to substitute with any yarns that will give you a similar gauge, taking care to choose yarns that are not too stretchy, or if they are, work a swatch and take your gauge while stretched. The most important measurement is the strap. See the fitting guides to make your calculations, and page thirty-five for how to make the bag fit on your right or left hip. And if you'd like to add a pouch, turn to page forty-one.

The Rolled Edge Sling has a serene quality.

Rolled Edge Sling Bag

This bag quietly shows off a seed stitch strap, a subtle herringbone effect, and a never-ending rolled edge. Like all things Moebius, these elements lend an unmistakable grace to the design, and are yours for remarkably little effort.

Yarn: Skacel Filo & Fili "India" (100% cotton, 50 g/ 38 m, 9 wpi), ivory, 6 balls; 1 yd waste yarn.

Needles: (you may require a different size to get correct gauge) size 10 (6 mm) circular 47" - 60" length, also 16" length

Notions: tapestry needle, stitch markers

Gauge: 15 sts = 4" (10 cm) after machine washing and drying

Finished size: 11" from rim to base, 10" wide. Strap 3" wide, 45" long (will stretch to approximately 48" when worn).

Fitting guide: Loop a tape measure around yourself, over one shoulder and falling at the opposite hip. Multiply this measurement by 2.7, and round off to the closest *even* number. This is your personal MCO number, and together with correct gauge, will give you a custom fit. Pattern as written is for a 48" strap (average woman).

Stitch Guide: See page 112 for abbreviations, page 110 - 111 for applied I-cord, page 109 for waste yarn and knitting with two circular needles.

Begin strap and rim

MCO 130 (or personal MCO number, see fitting guide). Place marker. *Purl 1, k1, repeat from * until marker reappears on *cable beneath needles*. Knit 30 with waste yarn, slide waste yarn loops back onto left needle, and with regular yarn, resume p1, k1 across the 30 waste yarn loops and onward, until 1 st remains before marker. Knit 1f&b in st before marker. This completes the first round. (261 sts) Knit 1, p1 for 7 rounds (marker appears between your *needles* 7 times). Knit 4 rounds, then bind off loosely.

Begin bag & work diagonal design

Because the waste yarn is placed in a k1p1 design instead of plain stockinette, you will have to look more carefully to identify the sts to be picked up. Place the 60 waste yarn sts on 16" needle, picking up 2 sts in each corner. (64 sts) Remove waste yarn. Place markers in center of each corner. (32 sts between markers) Knit 1 round. *Knit 1, ssk, k to within 3 sts of next marker, k2tog, k1, repeat from * once. Knit 1 round. (60 sts). *Knit 3, p3, repeat from * to first marker. Knit 2, *p3, k3, repeat from * to first marker, end k1. Knit 1, *p3, k3, repeat from * to first marker, end k2. Continue working rounds, shifting the 3 knits and 3 purls 1 st to the right after every round as established, for a total of 10 rounds. Knit 1 round.

Bag grows, then narrows and closes

Knit 3, k1f&b, repeat from * to first marker. (75 sts) Knit until bag measures 4.5" from end of diagonal design, increasing 1 st somewhere during this section. (76 sts total, 38 sts between markers) *Knit 1, ssk, k to within 3 sts of next marker, k2tog, k1, repeat from * once. Knit 1 round. Repeat last 2 rounds until 48 sts remain. Work 4 decrease rounds in a row. (32 sts) Turn bag inside out and either bind off and sew bottom or join with 3-needle bind-off. Weave in all ends.

Finish

Machine wash and dry the bag, or lay flat to dry.

CINNAMON BRAID SLING BAG

If you'd like a year-round bag beautiful enough to turn heads, this may be the one. The braid and long streams of purl ridges in oatmeal and molasses tones of thick cotton yarn have an almost carved quality. You may wonder how to work a sideways braid, but it's actually a special cable worked vertically. Like the other unfelted bags in this chapter, this one will stretch a little, allowing you to squeeze in a little more when you need to.

Yarn: Skacel Filo & Fili "India" (100% cotton, 50 g/ 38 m, 9 wpi), brown, 6 balls; 1 yd waste yarn.

Needles: (you may require a different size to get correct gauge) size 10 (6 mm) circular 47" - 60" length, also 16" length, optional 24" length

Notions: tapestry needle, stitch markers

Gauge: 15 sts = 4" (10 cm) after machine washing and drying

Finished size: 10" deep from rim to base, 8.5" wide. Strap 3" wide and 45" long (will stretch to approximately 48" when worn).

Fitting guide: Loop a tape measure around yourself like the strap of the sling bag, over one shoulder and falling at the opposite hip. Multiply this measurement by 3.1. This is your personal MCO number, and together with correct gauge, will give you a custom fit. Pattern as written is for a 48" strap (average woman).

Stitch Guide: See page 112 for abbreviations, page 110 - 111 for applied I-cord, page 109 for waste yarn and knitting with two circular needles.

Begin with strap and rim

MCO 150, (or personal MCO number, see fitting guide). Place marker. Knit 150 (or personal MCO number), k 30 with waste yarn, replace the 30 waste yarn loops on left needle, and use regular yarn to k over waste yarn loops. Knit to marker. This completes first round. Knit 2 more rounds. Purl 3 rounds. Knit 3 rounds.

Applied I-cord edge

Work applied I-cord until all sts are bound off. Graft or sew I-cord ends together.

Begin Bag

Place the 60 waste yarn sts on 16" or 24" needle, picking up 2 sts at each corner. (64 sts) Remove waste yarn. Place markers in center of each corner. (32 sts between markers) Begin knitting on the side which was purled. Complete this round and knit 32 more sts. The marker now between your needles marks the new beginning point. Purl 2 rounds. *Purl 1, p2tog, p to within 3 sts of next marker, p2tog, p1, repeat from * once. (60 sts)

Braid

The cabling rounds are rather tight to work, but the results will be worth it!

Knit 3 rounds. *Place 2 sts on cable needle and hold to *back* of work, k2, k2 sts from cable needle, repeat from * 14 times. Knit 2 rounds, then k 2 sts past first marker. *Place 2 sts on cable needle and hold to *front* of work, k2, k2 sts from cable needle, repeat from * 14 times. On the last round, you will work 2 sts past the marker.

Bag continues, then narrows and closes

Continue knitting rounds of 60 sts until bag measures 4.5" from last round of braid. *Knit 1, ssk, k to within 3 sts of next marker, k2tog, k1, repeat from * once. Knit 1 round. Repeat last 2 rounds until only 40 sts remain. Turn bag inside out and work 3-needle bind-off, or bind off and sew closed. Weave in all ends.

Finish

Machine wash and dry the bag, or lay flat to dry.

Linen Sling Bag

Linen, an ancient and durable fiber that appears in fairy tales as well as everyday life, makes a sling bag cool enough for a blazing summer and strong enough to last nearly forever! This design has two pouches, one sized for a cell phone or your keys, and the other big enough to hold larger items. Linen softens with washing, so don't hesitate to throw it in with your laundry again and again.

Yarn: Louet Euroflax Linen (100% wetspun linen, 100 g/ 270 yds, 22 wpi), robin's egg blue, 2 skeins; leaf green, 1 skein, 1 yd waste yarn

Needles: (you may require a different size to get correct gauge) size 9 (5.5 mm) circular, 47"- 60" length, also 16" length; also 10.5 (7 mm) needle for applied I-cord, may be straight or circular

Notions: tapestry needle, stitch markers

Gauge: (knit with double strand of yarn) 13 sts = 4" (10 cm) after washing and drying

Finished size: Bag is 12" deep from rim to base, 10" wide; larger pouch 7" deep, 6" wide; smaller pouch 4.5" deep, 3.25" wide; strap 48" long, 2" wide.

Fitting guide: Loop a tape measure around yourself, over one shoulder and falling at the opposite hip. Multiply this measurement by 2.9, and round off to the closest *even* number. This is your personal MCO number, and together with correct gauge, will give you a custom fit. Pattern as written is for a 48" strap (average woman).

Stitch Guide: See page 112 for abbreviations, page 110 - 111 for applied I-cord, page 109 for waste yarn and knitting with two circular needles. *Work with double strand of yarn throughout.*

Begin strap and rim

With double strand of yarn, MCO 140 (or personal MCO number, see fitting guide). Place marker. *Purl 1, k1, repeat from * until marker reappears on *cable beneath needles.* Knit 30 with waste yarn, slide waste yarn loops back onto left needle, and with regular yarn, resume p1, k1 pattern across the 30 waste yarn loops and onward, until 1 st remains before marker. Knit 1f&b in st before marker. This completes the first round. (301 sts) Knit 1, p1 for 3 rounds (marker appears between your *needles* 3 times).

Applied I-cord edge

With *larger* needle, work applied I-cord until all sts are bound off. Graft or sew I-cord ends together.

Begin bag

Because the waste yarn is placed in a k1, p1 design instead of plain stockinette, you will have to look more carefully to identify the sts to be picked up. Place the 60 waste yarn sts on 16" needle, picking up 3 sts in each corner. (66 sts) Remove waste yarn. Place markers between 2nd and 3rd st picked up in each corner. (33 sts between markers) Begin knitting on side which is 1 row shorter than other side, keeping to p1, k1 pattern (you are knitting one extra half-round on this side only, which balances sides). When you come to next marker, begin knitting all sts. You will now count rounds from this marker, so you may want to use a particular color marker to help you remember. Knit 1 full round of 66 sts. *Knit 1, ssk, k to 3 sts before next marker, k2tog, k1, repeat from * once. (62 sts) Knit 1 round. Repeat last 2 rounds twice. (54 sts)

Make openings for pouches

Larger pouch: *Knit 4, k next 19 sts with waste yarn, replace waste yarn sts on left needle and k over them with regular yarn, k to next marker. Smaller pouch: *Knit 7, k next 13 sts with waste yarn, replace waste yarn sts on left needle and k over them with regular yarn, k to first marker. Knit 3 rounds.

Tendril design

With double strand of green yarn, work 6-st repeat on the blue background. Take care to keep tension even as strands run behind the work. The 2-color rounds will be somewhat tighter than rest of work, and help shape the neck of the bag.

Bag continues

You may switch to 2 circular needles if you find it easier once the bag decreases near the bottom. Cut tail of green and continue working with double strand of blue. Knit 3 rounds. *Knit 4, k1f&b, repeat from *, end k4. (64 sts) Continue knitting until bag measures 4" from base of tendril design. *Knit 1, ssk, k to 3 sts before next marker, k2tog, k1, repeat from * once. Knit 1 round. Repeat last 2 rounds until 40 sts remain. Work 2 decrease rounds in a row. (32 sts). Turn bag inside out and work 3-needle bind-off, or bind off and sew together. Weave in all ends.

Pouches

If you'd like the pouches to be less bulky, knit first inch with double strand, then continue with single strand. Large pouch: with 16" needle, pick up 38 sts held by waste yarn, picking up 1 extra st in each corner. (40 sts) Remove waste yarn. With knit side facing you, use 2 strands of yarn held together to knit all 40 sts, placing a marker before each picked up corner st. (20 sts between markers) Continue knitting until pouch measures 5" from beginning. *As you decrease, you'll need to switch to 2 circular needles.* *Knit 1, ssk, k to 3 sts before next marker, k2tog, k1, repeat from * once. Knit 1 round. Repeat last 2 rounds until only 24 sts remain. Turn bag inside out and work 3-needle bind-off, or bind off and sew closed. Weave in all ends. Small pouch: Pick up 26 waste yarn sts plus 2 in each corner (30 sts) Continue as for large pouch, decreasing to 18 sts at end.

Finish

Machine wash and dry the bag. It will be softer after machine drying than if line dried, and may take several launderings to soften as much as you'd like.

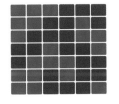

The tendril design is a 6-stitch repeat over 7 rounds.

Softie Sling Bag

This cotton ribbon yarn feels like a favorite T-shirt and knits up into a sling bag so soft that it may take you back to the days when you were three feet tall and carried your blankie everywhere. The arrow design on the strap and around the rim is a simple diagonal knit and purl pattern, which the Moebius generously rearranges into an arrow pattern. The arrow separates into the simple diagonal beneath the rim of the bag.

Yarn: Reynolds Cabaret (100% cotton, 30% rayon, 50 g/ 78 yds, 6 wpi), old rose, 2 skeins; antique blue and misty green, 1 skein each; 1 yd waste yarn

Needles: (you may require a different size to get correct gauge) size 8 (5 mm) circular, 47" – 60" length, also 16" length

Notions: tapestry needle, stitch markers

Gauge: 20 sts = 4" (10 cm) after machine washing and drying

Finished size: Bag is 9.5" deep from rim to base, 9" wide; strap 44" long, 2" wide. (Strap will stretch to about 48" when worn.)

Stitch Guide: See page 112 for abbreviations, page 110 - 111 for applied I-cord, page 109 for waste yarn and knitting with two circular needles.

Fitting guide: Loop a tape measure around yourself, over one shoulder and falling at the opposite hip. Multiply this measurement by 3.5, then round off to *a number that can be divided evenly by 6.* This is your personal MCO number, and together with correct gauge, will give you a custom fit. Pattern as written is for a 44" strap, which stretches to 48" (average woman).

Begin with strap

With rose, MCO 168 (or personal MCO number, see fitting guide). Place marker. *Knit 3, p3, repeat from * until marker appears on cable *beneath* needles, and sts on left needle are now mounted correctly, indicating completion of first half round. Knit 36 with waste yarn, replace waste yarn sts on left needle, then with regular yarn continue k3, p3 across the 36 waste yarn loops and on to marker. This completes first round. Purl 1, *k3, p3, repeat from * until 2 sts remain before marker, p2. Purl 2, *k3, p3, repeat from * until 1 st remains before marker, p1. *Purl 3, k3, repeat from * to marker. Knit 1, *p3, k3, repeat from until 2 sts remain before marker, k2. Knit 2, *p3, k3, repeat from until 1 st remains before marker, k1.

Applied I-cord edge

With blue, work applied I-cord until all sts are bound off. Graft or sew I-cord ends together.

Continue with bag

Because the waste yarn is placed in a k3, p3 design instead of plain stockinette, you will have to look more carefully to identify the sts to be picked up. Place the 72 waste yarn sts on 16" needle, picking up 2 sts in each corner. (76 sts) Remove waste yarn. Place markers in center of each corner. (38 sts between markers) Knit 1 full round. *Knit 1, ssk, k to 3 sts before next marker, k2tog, k1, repeat from * once. (72 sts) Knit 1 round. *Knit to 3 sts before next marker, k2tog, repeat from * once. (70 sts).

Begin leaf wreath design

With green and rose, work leaf wreath design. When design is complete, work increase round: *k2, k1f&b, k3, k1f&b, repeat from * to marker. (90 sts) Continue knitting until bag measures 7" from rim. *As you decrease, you'll need to switch to 2 circular needles.* *Knit 1, ssk, k to 3 sts before next marker, k2tog, k1, repeat from * once. (86 sts) Knit 1 round. Repeat last 2 rounds until 70 sts remain. Work decrease round every row until 42 sts remain.

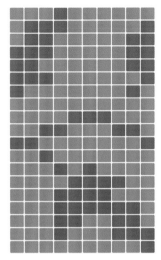

The leaf wreath design is a 10-stitch repeat over 19 rounds.

Finish

Turn bag inside out and work 3-needle bind-off, or bind off and sew bottom closed. Weave in all ends.

Yarn and design suggestions

You may substitute with any yarn which will give you similar gauge. Look for cottons, rayons, hemp, and other plant fibers, either alone or blended. If you cannot find a yarn that will give you similar gauge, think about combining two strands of thinner yarns. If you combine two different thinner yarns you may discover a very interesting fabric.

The Jester Bags are functional playthings with infinite possibilities, including the promise of enduring hilarity.

Antoinette Botsford, storyteller

Chapter Five - Jester tentacles bags

The first comment many people make upon seeing this playful Moebius creation is, "It looks alive!" Indeed, it seems as if it might have floated right out of a tide pool. And like undersea creatures who conceal pearls, the Jester Tentacles Bag hides its Moebius. Perhaps you can find the telltale half-twist in the close-up on page sixty, even before reading the caption which reveals where it is.

The Jester Tentacles Bag has one continuous edge and one continuous surface. Each bag sprouts lots of hidey-holes – an inner bag, tentacles, and hollow straps, but not a one of them truly has an inside or outside. They can't, for this creature is a pure-blooded Moebius.

Five steps to knit a Jester tentacles Bag

• Knit a Moebius band with two waste yarn openings, one wider than the other. After the first round, bind off with applied I-cord.

• Pick up the waste yarn stitches from the smaller opening, and knit the inner bag.

• Pick up waste yarn stitches from the larger opening, and knit the outer bag, adding waste yarn openings for the straps and tentacles.

• Pick up waste yarn stitches to knit the straps and tentacles.

• Felt, then shape by blowing up a balloon in each bag.

Mischievous as this bag may be, it is also perhaps the most practical design in the book. It's the ultimate "know-where-everything-is" purse, with so many little pockets for hiding keys, lipstick, pens, change for parking meters, grocery list, and wallet. It's also an instant cure for the blues – just wave your fingers inside the tentacles in public, and watch grins and giggles erupt around you.

If you're careful with the felting, and stop before the outer bag shrinks too much, you'll find that you can also wear the bag as a very jolly hat. I hope that you will knit one for a young person you love, and one for yourself, too. I also like to show people that the hat has a built-in bib! Just pull down the inner bag before putting it on.

Elaborations

Add tentacles to the tentacles (making waste yarn openings can become addictive), or add tentacles to the inner bag and let it hang outside like a marsupial marine baby, or add tentacles down the outer sides of the straps so that when you tie them under your chin (when worn as a hat), you look even more fetching. You could add colorful little bobbles (like barnacles) anywhere, and even if the barnacle yarn felts more slowly than the main yarn, the lumpy looseness of the barnacles will be tantalizing, like a tide pool full of life.

JESTER TENTACLES BAG

This bag has been described as the perfect anti-depressant, because it is not possible to encounter it without a grin. And by the time you put it on and slide your fingers into the tentacles, flipping them up and down, your grin may become a guffaw. In Puget Sound our sea stars (called starfish when I was a child) are bright purple or orange, and they and the bags are definitely kindred spirits. To knit one, you start with a narrow Moebius band and work two magical openings with five-stitch bridges separating them. The smaller opening becomes the inner bag and the larger becomes the outer bag, sprouting all those tentacles and straps. The Moebius half-twist nestles secretly along one bridge. You have to see it to believe it, but it works! The numerous "stretchings" of the outer bag into tentacles and straps all stay true to the one-surface nature of the Moebius.

Yarn: Cascade 220 (100% wool, 100 g/ 220 yds, 13 wpi) 3 skeins; 2 yds waste yarn in color A (for straps) and 3 yds in color B (for tentacles)

Needles: (you may require a different size to get correct gauge) size 10 (6 mm) circular, 47"- 60" length, also 16" length

Notions: tapestry needle, stitch markers

Gauge: (before felting) 14 sts = 4" (10 cm)

Finished size: Before felting, outer bag 26" around, length from rim to center base 10", strap 45". After felting, 21", 9", 36".

Stitch Guide: See page 112 for abbreviations, page 110 - 111 for applied I-cord, page 109 for waste yarn and knitting with two circular needles.

Begin Moebius band

MCO 70. Place marker and k 75. Use waste yarn A to knit the next 25 sts. Replace waste yarn sts on left needle and k 30 (the 25 waste yarn sts plus 5 more). Use waste yarn B to k next 35 sts. Replace on left needle and k35.

Finish edge with applied I-cord

Work applied I-cord around entire edge and weave ends together. This completes the rims of both inner and outer bags.

If you look closely at the two little bridges joining the inner and outer bags in this close-up, you'll see that one has a half-twist … that's the Moebius!

Work with two circular needles whenever there are too few stitches to fit around the 16" needle.

Inner Bag

Use 16" circular needle to pick up the 50 sts held on color A waste yarn. Remove waste yarn. With regular yarn, k 25, pick up and k 2 extra in corner, k25, pick up and k 3 extra in other corner, place marker. (55 sts) *Knit 4, k1f&b, repeat from * 10 times. (66 sts) Knit 33, place second marker, k to first marker. Knit until bag measures 6" from rim. *Knit 1, ssk, k to within 3 sts of next marker, k2tog, k1, repeat from * once. (62 sts) Knit 1 round. Repeat last 2 rounds twice more. (54 sts) Close bottom with 3-needle bind-off, or bind off and sew together.

Outer Bag

Use 16" circular needle to pick up 70 sts held on color B waste yarn. Remove waste yarn. The inner bag should hang inside the circle of needles, suspended from each end. With regular yarn, k35, pick up and k 2 extra in corner, k35, pick up and k 3 extra in second corner. (75 sts) Place marker. *Knit 4, k1f&b, repeat from * 14 times. (90 sts) Knit 5 rounds. Eight sts before end of 5th round, use waste yarn A to k a 15-st waste yarn section. Replace waste yarn sts on left needle and k 45 (15 waste yarn sts plus 30 sts). Use waste yarn A to knit second 15-st waste yarn section. K 53 (15 waste yarn sts plus 38 sts, stopping at marker). *These two color A waste yarn sections will become the straps of your bag.* Knit 5 rounds. In next round, work 3 color B waste yarn sections of 11 - 15 sts each, spaced approximately one third of the way apart. *Do not* be precise and do not make

them exactly the same size or you will ruin the effect. Knit 7 rounds. Work between 3 and 5 color B waste yarn sections of 9 - 13 sts each where you like. *Do not* be symmetrical and do not make them exactly the same size. Trust this, and you will find that allowing the natural flow of things blesses you with grace and beauty which the logical mind cannot fathom. Continue knitting until bag measures 5" long from top of rim. *Knit 7, k2tog, repeat from * 9 times. (80 sts) Knit 5 rounds. *Knit 6, k2tog, repeat from * 9 times. (70 sts) Knit 5 rounds. *Knit 5, k2tog, repeat from * 9 times. (60 sts) Knit 4 rounds. *Knit 4, k2tog, repeat from * 9 times. (50 sts) Knit 2 rounds. *Knit 3, k2tog, repeat from * 9 times. (40 sts) Knit 1 round. *Knit 2, k2tog, repeat from * 9 times. (30 sts) Knit 1 round. *Knit 1, k2tog, repeat from * 9 times. (20 sts) Cut yarn, thread needle, and pull yarn snugly through all sts, secure, and weave in ends.

Straps

Pick up all sts in one color A waste yarn section, adding 2 picked up sts at each corner. Knit all rounds, knitting 2 tog on each needle every 6 rounds. Vary placement of the k2tog's, at beginning, middle, or end of each needle. When 3 sts remain on each needle, place all 6 on one needle and work as I-cord: *k6, replace all 6 sts on left needle, and repeat from * until strap is 45" long. *Knit 2tog, k to end, replace on left needle, repeat from * until only 3 sts remain. Cut yarn and use tapestry needle to weave through sts and weave in end. Make second strap same as first.

Jester Tentacles

Work each color B waste yarn section one at a time. When you pick up the sts, pick up 2 extras in each corner. Knit for about an inch, then begin decreasing same as for the straps. Finally work your way down to 4 sts, then 2, then k2tog, cut the yarn, and weave in ends. Make the jester tentacles different lengths and widths, without being analytical about it! After all, soon you'll be filling the tentacles with lip gloss, a pen, your keys, a spoon for your yogurt, and your marbles if you haven't already lost them. So relax, and enjoy bringing such a happy creature into the world.

Liberated method of tentacle-creation

If you would like this bag to really resemble a sea creature about to wave a tentacle and pull you into the sea, skip the color B waste yarn sections, and finish the bag as written, but don't felt yet. Now begin adding tentacles at whim by opening up magic openings. Just run a circular needle through a line of stitches where you want to place a tentacle, catching one side of each stitch as you go. Skip down one line of stitches and run a second circular needle through the next line of stitches. Now horror of horrors and oh what freedom! Snip a strand of yarn in the line of stitches between the two needle-held lines, and unravel it just to the edges of the held stitches. Get your ball of yarn and begin knitting your picked-up stitches, adding 2-3 stitches at the corners. You must add an extra stitch because unlike a waste yarn opening, you have actually lost a row of real knitting between the picked up stitches.

As you will see if you try this liberated method of tentacle-creation, it frees you to add appendages wherever they really seem to be wanted by the creature in your hands. I encourage you to listen to this curious being you are knitting. You may hear a small voice telling you where it wants the next tentacle, and how long it should be. And there's nothing stopping you from adding a small tentacle or two on the handle – after all, you can make a magic opening anywhere you have lines of stitches to liberate! And the larger tentacles might like to sprout little tentacles … there are no limits.

Felting

Felt according to general instructions on pages 16 - 19. If you see any weak spots where tentacles or straps begin, reinforce them before felting. I felted my bag for only 5 minutes, checking after 3. If you'd like the bag to be floppy, felt it very lightly; if you'd prefer more body, and don't mind it being a bit smaller, let it go longer. Check it often! I let mine go through the spin cycle, pulled and patted the straps and tentacles into shape, giving them an encouraging tweak in the directions they wanted to curl, and blew up a balloon inside both inner and outer bags to give them a lovely swollen shape. If you suspend the balloon-filled creature by the straps, it will appear that an octopus is swimming through the sea of your home.

JESTER TENTACLES HAT

Simply stop the felting process when it fits the intended head (which must be nearby). The inner bag may be stuffed inside the hat … or pulled down to create a hat with a bib! There are few things you can be sure of in life, but you may rest assured that this hat will generate jolliness.

Our local sea stars are close relatives of the Jester Tentacles Bags. I photographed these on Madrona Point, a sacred preserve on nearby Orcas Island.

Child's Jester Tentacles Bag

Here is a kid-size version of the Jester Tentacles Bag, with the added pizazz of random splashes of color. The inner pouch is shaped like a ball, allowing for rings of color with a colored circle at its heart. There is no rhyme or reason to the color changes I made, and I am leaving you to make your own. Please change colors with gleeful abandon, which matches the exuberant spirit of sea stars, Jester Tentacles Bag, and children, and I suspect it matches your spirit as well, if you are knitting it.

Yarn: Cascade 220 (100% wool, 100 g/ 220 yds, 13 wpi) about 2 skeins total in various colors (or one color if desired); 2 yds waste yarn in color A and 3 yds in color B

Needles: (you may require a different size to get correct gauge) size 10 (6 mm) circular, 47"- 60" length, also 16" length

Notions: tapestry needle, stitch markers

Gauge: (before felting) 14 sts = 4" (10 cm)

Finished size: Before felting, bag is 22' around, length from rim to center base 9.5", strap 35" long. After felting, 18", 7", 28".

Stitch Guide: See page 112 for abbreviations, pages 110 - 111 for applied I-cord, page 109 for waste yarn and knitting with two circular needles.

Begin with a Moebius band

With main color, MCO 55. Place marker and k 60 (first half-round plus 5 sts). Use waste yarn A to k next 18 sts. Replace waste yarn sts on left needle and k 23 (the 18 waste yarn sts plus 5 more). Use waste yarn B to k next 27 sts. Replace on left needle and k27 (end at the marker). Finish edge with applied I-cord.

Inner Bag

Use two circular needles whenever there are too few stitches to fit around the 16" needle. Use 16" circular needle to pick up (but not knit) the 36 sts held on color A waste yarn. Remove waste yarn. With main color, *k18, pick up and k 2 extra sts in corner, repeat from * once, place marker. (40 sts) *Knit 4, k1f&b, repeat from * 7 times. (48 sts) Knit until inner bag measures 2.5" long. *Knit 4, k2tog, repeat from * to marker. (40 sts) Knit 3 rounds. *Knit 3, k2tog, repeat from * to marker. (32 sts) Knit 3 rounds. *Knit 2, k2tog, repeat from * to marker. (24 sts) Knit 2 rounds. *Knit 1, k2tog, repeat from * to marker. (16 sts) Knit 1 round. *Knit 2tog, repeat from * to marker. (8 sts) Cut tail, use tapestry needle to weave through remaining 8 sts and weave in ends.

Outer Bag

Use 16" circular needle to pick up (but not knit) 54 sts on color B waste yarn. Remove waste yarn. The inner bag should hang inside the circle of needles, suspended from each end.

With regular yarn, place marker, k27, pick up and k 3 extra sts in corner, k27, pick up and k 3 extra sts in second corner. (60 sts) Place marker. *Knit 4, k1f&b, repeat from * 11 times. (72 sts) Knit 5 rounds. 7 sts before end of fifth round, use waste yarn A to k a 14-st waste yarn section. Replace waste yarn sts on left needle and k 36 (14 waste yarn sts plus 22 regular). Use waste yarn A to work another 14-st waste yarn section. K 43 (14 waste yarn sts plus 29 regular, stopping at marker). *These two color A waste yarn sections will become the straps.* Knit 4 rounds. In next round, work 3 color B waste yarn sections of 11 - 15 sts each, spaced approximately one third of the way apart. *Do not* be precise and do not make them exactly the same size or you will ruin the effect. Knit 6 rounds. Work 3 - 5 color B waste yarn sections of 9 - 13 sts each where you want them. *Do not* be symmetrical and do not make them exactly the same size or you will ruin the effect. Trust this, and you will find that allowing the natural flow of things blesses you with grace and beauty which the logical mind cannot fathom. Continue knitting until bag measures 5" from top of rim. Begin decreases: *k 7, k2tog, repeat from * to first marker. (64 sts) Knit 5 rounds.

*Knit 6, k2tog, repeat from * to first marker. (56 sts) Knit 5 rounds. *Knit 5, k2tog, repeat from to first marker. (48 sts) Knit 4 rounds. *Knit 4, k2tog, repeat from * to first marker. (40 sts) Knit 2 rounds. *Knit 3, k2tog, repeat from * to first marker. (32 sts) Knit 1 round. *Knit 2, k2tog, repeat from * to first marker. (24 sts) Knit 1 round. *Knit 1, k2tog, repeat from * to first marker. (16 sts) Cut yarn, thread needle, and pull yarn snugly through all sts, secure, and weave in all ends.

Straps and tentacles

Follow instructions for adult size bag, but make straps 35" long, adding rounds of other colors as desired.

Felting and finishing

Follow instructions for adult size bag.

CHAPTER SIX - MOEBIUS BOWLS & KITTY NEST

These bowls are imbued with a radiance best seen and felt while you hold them, silent and empty. Later you can fill them with anything you like, perhaps hot rolls wrapped in a tea towel, where they will stay warm and fragrant through your meal. I keep one bowl beside my knitting chair, holding small tools and my current small project, another on the floor, to hold my working yarn so it doesn't roll away, and several others are piled with colorful balls of yarn. A white bowl on my table looks resplendent, filled with tangerines, pomegranates, and green apples. You might knit one for your bathroom to hold hand towels, or your sea shell collection. There's a larger bowl as well, which makes a fine home for a small cat or a pair of kittens, somewhere to curl up during those first days away from mom.

*Crystal Palace
"Iceland,"
filled with a skein
of Fleece Artist
"Curly Locks."*

STEPS FOR MAKING A MOEBIUS BOWL

- Knit a Moebius band for the rim, and finish it with applied I-cord.

- Pick up stitches beneath the I-cord and knit the bowl downward.

- Add fringe (optional), and felt.

- Add cat, yarn – or both!

Fringed Felted Moebius Bowl

After I'd taken my first felted Moebius bowl from the washing machine, shaped it, and patted the fringe into place, I stood back and beamed. It seemed reminiscent of many things I love: Native American designs, pottery, a bird's best, a hearth. I have fantasies of making one large enough to curl up in myself, but it would take a very big washing machine to felt it.

Yarn: Crystal Palace Iceland (100% wool, 100 g/ 109 yards, 7 wpi), ice blue, 3 skeins; *or* Wool in the Woods Sophia (50% wool, 50% llama, 170 g/ 200 yds, 9 wpi), 2 skeins pastel

Needles: (you may require a different size to get correct gauge) size 11 (8 mm) circular, length 47" - 60", also a shorter length, between 24"–36"

Notions: tapestry needle, stitch markers

Gauge: (before felting) 13 sts = 4" (10 cm)

Finished size: Before felting, rim is 2.5" wide and 36" around, belly 43" around, 18" from rim to center base. After felting, rim 1.75" and 26", belly 30", rim to center base 9.5".

Wool in the Woods "Sophia," filled with a Fleece Artist Thrum Mitts kit.

Stitch Guide: See page 112 for abbreviations, page 110 - 111 for applied I-cord, page 109 for waste yarn and knitting with two circular needles, and page 108 for turning a Moebius band into a simple circle.

Begin with Moebius rim

With longer needle, MCO 100. Place marker. *Knit 1 round, p 1 round, repeat from * twice. Bind off all edge sts with applied I-cord, graft or sew ends together, and weave in yarn ends.

Start bowl

With shorter needle, pick up 100 sts directly beneath I-cord edge, 1 st for each I-cord st above. This will bring you halfway around the edge of the rim, allowing the 2 needle tips to join and knit in the round without any twist, leaving the half-twist of the Moebius rim hanging beneath the stitches on your needle. Place marker and k 5 rounds. *Knit 2, k1f&b, repeat from *, end k1. (133 sts) Knit 12 rounds. *Knit 8, k2 tog, repeat from *, end k3. (120 sts) Knit 4 rounds. *Knit 8, k2tog, repeat from * to marker. (108 sts) Knit 4 rounds. *Knit 7, k2tog, repeat from * to marker. (96 sts) Knit 4 rounds.

Base of bowl

*Knit 6, k2tog, repeat from *. (84 sts) Knit 3 rounds. *Knit 5, k2tog, repeat from *. (72 sts) Knit 2 rounds. *Knit 4, k2tog, repeat from *. (60 sts) Knit 2 rounds. *Knit 3, k2tog, repeat from *. (48 sts) Knit 2 rounds. *Knit 2, k2tog, repeat from *. (36 sts) Knit 2 rounds. *Knit 1, k2tog, repeat from *. (24 sts) Knit 1 round. Knit 2 tog all the way around. (12 sts) Knit 1 round. Knit 2 tog all the way around. (6 sts) Cut tail and use tapestry needle to thread end through the 6 sts, pull tight and secure. Weave in all ends.

Applying Fringe

Cut approximately fifty 11" lengths of yarn and attach them every other st immediately below lower I-cord rim. To attach fringe, fold a piece of yarn in half, insert crochet hook through st where you wish to attach fringe, hook the loop formed by the folded yarn with the crochet hook, and pull halfway through st. Use crochet hook or fingers to pull the yarn ends through the loop and tug ends down firmly to form a knot.

Felting and finishing

Felt according to general instructions on pages 16-19. Check the fringe every minute and pull the strands apart if they are matting together. After ten minutes, you can begin to check the fringe less frequently. If towards the end it seems that the fringe is longer than you'd like, you must trim it while it still has time to feather at the ends, or it will look like a bad hair cut! Felt the bowl thoroughly so it is very firm. When done, blow a balloon up inside the bowl, and let it dry with the balloon inside, to give it a smooth curved shape.

Yarn and design suggestions

Make sure the yarn you choose will felt substantially, for the bowl must hold its shape without going limp. Any of the yarns used for felting projects in either *Treasury* will do very well. The distinct colors of variegated yarns show up especially well in the fringe, but blur in the felted fabric itself, which is lovely. You could add a handle to the bowl and use it as a shopping basket, or replace the fringe with a series of small knitted pouches to hold knitting accessories like tapestry needles, measuring tapes, cable needles, and markers. The possibilities are endless.

This Moebius Bowl took 2 skeins of Cascade Pastaza (50% llama, 50% wool, 100 g/ 132 yds), and holds a hand-painted skein of Wool in the Woods "Frost."

LARGE BOWL OR KITTY NEST

Who knows who or what will curl up in this Moebius nest – a pair of kittens, a puppy, or a knitting project? Follow the directions for the previous pattern, with changes in the following sections:

Yarn: 4 skeins of Crystal Palace Iceland in color "Tundra."

Finished size: Before felting, rim 2.5" wide, 48" around, belly 54" around, body 20" from rim to center base. After felting, rim 1.75" wide, 32" around, belly 38", body 11".

Little Mishka has returned to the womb.

Begin with Moebius rim
MCO 125.

Begin bowl
With shorter needle, pick up 125 sts directly beneath I-cord edge. Place marker and k 5 rounds. *Knit 2, k1f&b, repeat from *, end k2. (166 sts) Knit 15 rounds. *Knit 8, k2 tog, repeat from *, end k 6. (150 sts) Knit 4 rounds. *Knit 8, k2tog, repeat from *. (135 sts) Knit 5 rounds. *Knit 6, k2tog, repeat from *, end k7. (119 sts) Knit 4 rounds. *Knit 8, k2tog, repeat from *, end k9. (108 sts) Knit 4 rounds. *Knit 7, k2tog, repeat from *end. (96 sts) Knit 4 rounds.

Base of bowl
*Knit 4, k2tog, repeat from *. (80 sts). Knit 3 rounds. *Knit 6, k2tog, repeat from *. (70 sts). Knit 3 rounds. *Knit 5, k2tog, repeat from *. (60 sts). Knit 3 rounds. *Knit 4, k2tog, repeat from *. (50 sts). Knit 3 rounds. *Knit 3, k2tog, repeat from *. (40 sts). Knit 3 rounds. *Knit 3, k2tog, repeat from *. (32 sts). Knit 2 rounds. *Knit 2, k2tog, repeat from *. (24 sts). Knit 2 rounds. *Knit 2tog, repeat from *. (12 sts). Knit 1 round. *Knit 2tog, repeat from *. (6 sts). Cut tail and use tapestry needle to thread end through the 6 sts, pull tight and secure. Weave in all ends.

Fringe
Cut approximately sixty-five 11" lengths of yarn and follow directions in previous pattern.

I feel as if I'm in a museum of prehistoric pottery.
visitor at a Magical Knitting Show

Chapter Seven - Moebius Clusters

Looking at and knitting the pieces in this chapter fills me with delight, and I have fond memories of how I encountered each one in its infancy. The Fanny Basket to the right was the offspring of my realization that baskets need not have just one compartment, but could have two. The design worked on the first try, but played a bit of a trick on me. I had no idea that dual curvaceous compartments would look so much like a part of the human anatomy. The Canadian name is the Bum Basket, in the States it's a Fanny Basket, but mostly, everyone ends up calling it by the most obvious name (pardon my French), the Moebiass. It is certain to bring much merriment to your home and workplace.

Well, I thought after that, if I can make two compartments, I could probably make four! And as you can see to the right, the Moebius basket can be subdivided into four compartments as well. It's a great way to display your favorite fiber tools, or it may be filled with small glass jars and hold fresh flowers.

Then I embarked on an entirely different venture, as described in the first *Treasury*, of attempting to execute a Moebius Magic trick with my knitting needles. You see, if you take a paper Moebius band, and draw two parallel lines down its length (like a three-lane road), you'll discover several things.

First, you cannot draw a pair of lines, but only one continuous line, and second, when you take scissors and cut along this line which seems to have a mind of its own, the Moebius band unravels into a single narrow Moebius band, one third the width of the original, with another narrow band twice-as-long (and also one-third-as-wide) as the original, looped through the first band. And the twice-as-long band is not a Moebius, alas, for it has two sides and two full twists. Unless you are a genius, you can't possibly follow what I have said, so please sit down and do it, and enjoy seeing what happens.

So I set about to translate this trick into knitting, employing certain magical devices like waste yarn where the two bands needed to come apart. Unfortunately I unwittingly inserted two extra crossings at the very beginning and the three twists multiplied themselves approximately threefold, which meant I had more twists than I could possibly sort out. I think even Harry Houdini would have been bamboozled.

After a good night's sleep, I realized with considerable glee that the troublesome extra crossings were the necessary magical element to connect a set of three nesting Moebius Baskets, all with one single continuous edge and surface. As happens so often, a "failure" had opened a window into a wonderful new vista.

And the original mistake – well, so many knitters, as well as non-knitters, among them aeronautical engineers, artificial intelligence scientists, and children, insisted I include it, that I gave in, and so you will find instructions to make your own mistake, or its correct version, at the end of this chapter. It's easy to recognize the correct version, because it's being modeled by a horse.

Moebius Fanny Basket (U.S.)
Moebius Bum Basket (Canada)
Moebiass (pardon my French)

This demure saddlebag-style Moebius basket surprised me and will surprise you and your friends. In fact, it may help you make new friends. I swear my intentions were innocent. All I wanted to do was try a two-compartment Moebius, and I really like pink and green together . . . when it came out of the washing machine I suddenly recognized what I had created! I shall leave you to your own anatomical analysis while I point out that this basket has but one edge (although it is a little edgier than my other designs, I admit) and only one surface. You can climb up the side and along the handle, fall inside, and swoop back up and over the divider, exploring the "insides" of both compartments, then climb back up the handle and fall outside. Endlessly. I plan to take one to a topologist's convention someday, and offer it as the booby prize to those nuts.

Yarn: Cascade 220 (100% wool, 220 yds/ 100 g, 13 wpi), pink, 2 skeins; pale green, 1 skein; 2 pieces waste yarn in contrasting colors (referred to as A and B).

Needles: (you may require a different size to get correct gauge) size 11 (8 mm) circular, 47" and 16" lengths

Notions: tapestry needle, stitch markers

Gauge: (before felting) 12 sts = 4" (10 cm) with double strand of yarn

Finished size: Before felting: handle is 2" wide, 10" long, rim 23" around, each belly 21" around and 9.5" from rim to base. After felting, handle 1.25" wide, 7.5" long, rim 18", each belly 17", and height 6.5".

Stitch Guide: See page 112 for abbreviations, pages 110 - 111 for applied I-cord, page 109 for waste yarn and knitting with two circular needles. *Knit with a double strand of yarn throughout.*

Begin with handle and rim

With double strand of green, MCO 56. Knit 28. With color A waste yarn, k next 28 sts. Slide the 28 waste yarn sts back to left needle, and resume knitting with regular yarn. Knit 56 (first 28 loops are waste yarn, second 28 are regular). With color B waste yarn, k next 28 sts. Slide the 28 waste yarn sts back to left needle, and with regular yarn, knit over waste yarn loops to marker. Purl 1 round. Knit 1 round. Finish edge with applied I-cord. Weave or sew ends together. This completes basket handle and rim.

First compartment

Use 16" circular needle to pick up the 56 sts held by color A waste yarn. Remove waste yarn. Using double strand of green and beginning above the color B waste yarn section, working above it from right to left, place marker, *k first 28 sts, pick up and k 1 extra st, repeat from * once. (58 sts) *From this point, instructions are for both compartments.*

*Knit 2, k2tog, repeat from * 6 times. Place marker, k 30. (51 sts) K 21, *k2, k1f&b, repeat from * 9 times. (61 sts) Cut tail of green. With double strand of pink, k 12 rounds. *Switch to 2 circular needles when sts are too crowded for single needle.* Knit 22, k2tog, *k3, k2tog, repeat from * 6 times, k2. (53 sts) Knit 5 rounds. Knit 20, k2tog, *k3, k2tog, repeat from * 5 times, k1. (46 sts) Knit 5 rounds. Knit 20, k2tog, *k2, k2tog, repeat from * 5 times. (39 sts) Knit 3 rounds. *Knit 4, k2 tog, repeat from * 5 times, end k3. (33 sts) Knit 1 round. *K 1, k2tog, repeat from *. (22 sts) Knit 1 round. *K 2tog, repeat from * to end. (11 sts) Cut tail, thread through all sts and pull closed. Weave in the end.

Second compartment

Use 16" circular needle to pick up (but not knit) the 56 sts held by color B waste yarn. Remove waste yarn. With right side of work facing you, begin knitting with a double strand of green yarn along green rim of first compartment (this is the center rim that divides the compartments), going from right to left. Place marker, k first 28 sts, pick up and k 1 extra, k 28, pick up and k 1 extra. (58 sts) *From here continue with previous instructions.* You will find that the 28 rim sts on your needle are grouped in oddly twisted sets of three caused by the decreases made when the first compartment was knit. Make sure to work each st separately within these sets. Don't be concerned about making it look just right, for once felted,

the green rim will be smooth. Now knit the second compartment the same as the first.

Felting and finishing

Weave in all ends, taking special care to weave through any loose areas near handles. Felt according to general instructions on pages 16-19. Pat and pull into desired shape, and let dry.

Yarn and design suggestions

You could choose to make this lovely piece in any skin tone (perhaps a collection representing all of humanity?) or may prefer to use colors which disguise the basket's anatomical eloquence, instead allowing its graceful form to express itself in an anatomically anonymous manner. Think of it as a small market basket! Do be certain to use yarn that will felt firmly enough to give the basket body. While you're choosing colors, be creative - you could make the basket all one color, or make each cheek, ahem, I mean compartment, a different color; work stripes, duplicate stitch a little tattoo . . . I think I'd best stop while I'm behind.

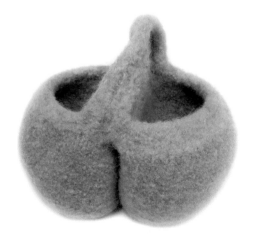

Nesting Moebius Trio

These three connected bowls have only one side and one edge – a single Moebius with three "swellings." You can make nesting Moebii in sets of three, five, seven - any odd number. If the number were even, you'd end up with two edges and two surfaces; not a Moebius and not magical. The bowls are graduated in size and may be nested inside one another. What's the trick? You must establish three crossings before beginning to knit your MCO (see page 96).

Yarn: Manos del Uruguay, (100% wool, 100 g/ 138 yds, 8.5 wpi), deep blue, 2 skeins; blue-gold multi, 1 skein; 3 pieces waste yarn.

Needles: (you may require a different size to get correct gauge) size 11 (8 mm) circular, 47" - 60" length, also 16" length

Notions: tapestry needle, stitch markers, 3 safety pins

Gauge: (before felting) 12 sts = 4" (10 cm)

Finished size: Before felting: handles 1.5" wide, 11.5" long, rims 22", 20", 18" around, bellies 26", 23", 20" around, height 10", 9", and 8" from rim to base. After felting, handles 1" wide, 6.5" long, rims 13", 12", 11", bellies 19", 17.5", 16", and height 6", 5.5", 5".

Stitch Guide: See page 112 for abbreviations, page 110 - 111 for applied I-cord, page 109 for waste yarn and knitting with two circular needles.

Begin with bowl handles and rims

With blue yarn and longer needle, MCO 156. *See page 96 for how to set up 3 crossings during the MCO, which creates 3 half-twists, one to go in between each of the 3 handles.* Place marker and k184. Use waste yarn to k next 28 sts. Slide the 28 waste yarn sts back to left needle and k across 28 waste yarn sts using regular yarn. Knit 28. Use second piece of waste yarn to k next 24 sts. Slide 24 waste yarn sts back to left needle and k across waste yarn sts with regular yarn. Knit 28. Use third piece of waste yarn to k next 20 sts. Slide 20 waste yarn sts back to left needle and k across 20 waste yarn sts with regular yarn, ending at marker. Purl 1 round. Cut tail of yarn. With blue-gold yarn, finish edge with applied I-cord. Weave or sew ends together. This completes bowl handles and rims.

Mark right sides

Take the Moebius band and lay it out so it resembles one of the mirror reflections at the top of page 97, with a line of waste yarn appearing in each flat section between the twists. Attach a safety pin beside the middle of each waste yarn line. This identifies the three "right sides" where openings for the bowls will be. When knitting the bowls, make sure to work facing the right side.

Largest bowl

Switch to using two circular needles when there are too few stitches to fit on the 16" circular.

Use 16" circular needle to pick up the stitches held by the longest waste yarn section, which has 28 sts on each side, for a total of 56. Remove waste yarn. Using blue yarn, place marker, and k first 28 sts, pick up and k 1 extra, k 28, pick up and k 1 extra. (58 sts) *Knit 2, k1f&b, repeat from *, end k1. (77 sts) *Knit 24, k1f&b, repeat from *, end k2. (80 sts) Knit 12 rounds. *Knit 6, k2tog, repeat from *. (70 sts) Knit 4 rounds. *Knit 5, k2tog, repeat from *. (60 sts) Knit 4 rounds. *Knit 4, k2tog, repeat from *. (50 sts) Knit 4 rounds. *Knit 3, k2tog, repeat from *. (40 sts) Knit 1 round. *Knit 3, k2tog, repeat from *. (32 sts) Knit 1 round. *Knit 2, k2tog, repeat from *. (24 sts) Knit 1 round. *Knit 1, k2tog, repeat from *. (16 sts) Knit 1 round. *Knit 2tog, repeat from *. (8 sts) Cut tail, thread through all sts and pull closed. Weave in the end.

Middle bowl

Pick up waste yarn sts same as for biggest basket, this time 24 on each side for a total of 48. Using blue yarn, k first 24 sts, pick up and k 1 extra, k next 24, pick up and k 1 extra. (50 sts) *Knit 2, k1f&b, repeat from *, end k2. (66 sts) *Knit 15, k1f&b, repeat from *, end k2. (70 sts) Knit 12 rounds. *Knit 5, k2tog, repeat from *. (60 sts) Knit 4 rounds. *Knit 4, k2tog, repeat from *. (50 sts)

Knit 4 rounds. *Knit 3, k2tog, repeat from *. (40 sts) Knit 1 round. *Knit 3, k2tog, repeat from *. (32 sts) Knit 1 round. *Knit 2, k2tog, repeat from *. (24 sts) Knit 1 round. *Knit 1, k2tog, repeat from *. (16 sts) Knit 1 round. *Knit 2tog, repeat from *. (8 sts) Cut tail, thread through all sts and pull closed. Weave in the end.

Smallest bowl

Pick up waste yarn sts same as for biggest basket, this time 20 on each side for a total of 40. Using blue yarn, k first 20 sts, pick up and k 1 extra, k next 20, pick up and k 1 extra. (42 sts) *Knit 2, k1f&b, repeat from *. (56 sts) *Knit 13, k1f&b, repeat from *. (60 sts) Knit 8 rounds. *Knit 4, k2tog, repeat from *. (50 sts) Knit 4 rounds. *Knit 3, k2tog, repeat from *. (40 sts) Knit 1 round. *Knit 3, k2tog, repeat from *. (32 sts) Knit 1 round. *Knit 2, k2tog, repeat from *. (24 sts) Knit 1 round. *Knit 1, k2tog, repeat from *. (16 sts) Knit 1 round. *Knit 2tog, repeat from *. (8 sts) Cut tail, thread through all sts and pull closed. Weave in the end.

Felting and finishing

Felt according to general instructions on pages 16-19. During felting, the bowl may turn themselves inside out. If so, rotate until there is just the one half-turn in each handle. When correct, each handle has one half twist and no more, as shown. Don't become discouraged, as this trickster trio almost never falls into the correct position until you fiddle for a bit.

Felted Foursome

This wondrous construction has but one surface and one edge, like all the other Moebius baskets. I just had to add more waste yarn openings to see what happened! This design begins like a very large Moebius basket, but after picking up the waste yarn stitches of the opening, you knit four new waste yarn openings along its circumference. Each opening will become a pouch, and the four pouches will be joined at the center before felting. You may find yourself a little disoriented until you've gone far enough to see what you're making, but fear not; keep knitting and soon you shall have your very own Felted Foursome. My test knitters tell me they fill their Felted Foursomes with all sorts of things: cutlery and napkins for picnics, knitting needle displays in yarn shops, flower arrangements, and rolled guest towels for the bathroom.

Yarn: Araucania Nature Wool (100% wool, 100 g/ 242 yds, 12 wpi), red, 2 skeins; indigo, 1 skein; 5 pieces waste yarn

Needles: (you may require a different size to get correct gauge) size 11 (8 mm) circular, 47" - 60", 24"– 32", and 16" lengths

Notions: tapestry needle, stitch markers

Gauge: (before felting) 14 sts = 4" (10 cm) with double strand of yarn.

Finished size: Before felting: handle 2" wide, 10" long, rim 21" around, each belly 23" around and 9.5" from rim to base. After felting, handle 1.25" wide, 7.5" long, rim 16", each belly 19", rim to base 6.5".

Stitch Guide: See page 112 for abbreviations, page 110 - 111 for applied I-cord, page 109 for waste yarn and knitting with two circular needles. *Knit with a double strand of yarn throughout.*

Begin with handle and outer rim

With longer needle and double strand of indigo, MCO 100. Place marker and k 135. Use waste yarn to knit next 65 sts. Replace the 65 waste yarn sts on left needle, k across the 65 sts with regular yarn, ending at marker. Purl 1 round, k 1 round. Reverse direction of work and k 65. Finish edge with applied I-cord. Weave or sew ends together. This completes handle and outer rim.

Inner rim and pouch openings

Use the mid-length circular needle to pick up the 130 sts held in the waste yarn section. Remove waste yarn. With indigo, pick up and p 2 sts in first corner of opening, p1. Purl next 30 sts with new waste yarn, replace these sts on left needle and p over them with regular yarn. Purl next 3 sts with regular yarn. Purl next 30 sts with new waste yarn, replace these sts on left needle and p over them with regular yarn. Purl 1, pick up and p 2 sts at corner of opening, p1. Purl next 30 sts with new waste yarn, replace these sts on left needle and p over them with regular yarn. Purl 3 more with regular yarn. Purl next 30 sts with new waste yarn, replace these sts on left needle and p over them with regular yarn, p 1. (134 sts) Place marker. Knit 1 round, p 1 round, k 1 round. Finish edge with applied I-cord. This completes inner rim.

First pouch

Switch to using two circular needles when there are too few stitches to fit on the 16" circular.

Use shortest circular needle to pick up the 60 sts waste yarn from 1 of the 4 sections. Remove waste yarn. With red, pick up and k1 in corner, k30, pick up and k1 in other corner, k30. Place marker. (62 sts) Knit 20 rounds. *Knit 4, k2tog, repeat from *, end k2. (52 sts) Knit 4 rounds. *Knit 5, k2tog, repeat from *, end k3. (45 sts) Knit 4 rounds. *Knit 7, k2tog, repeat from *. (40 sts) Knit 3 rounds. *Knit 6, k2tog, repeat from *. (35 sts) Knit 1 round. *Knit 5, k2tog, repeat from *. (30 sts) Knit 1 round.

*Knit 4, k2tog, repeat from *. (25 sts) Knit 1 round. *Knit 3, k2tog, repeat from *. (20 sts) Knit 1 round. *Knit 2, k2tog, repeat from *. (15 sts) *Knit 1, k2tog, repeat from *. (10 sts) Cut tail, thread through all sts and pull closed. Weave in the end.

Second, third, and fourth pouches

Repeat instructions for first pouch, taking care to maintain right sides to match the first pouch.

Finishing and felting

Before felting, fold inner side of each pouch in half so 4 corners meet in middle of the basket, forming an "X". Loosely sew center points together, then loosely sew each adjacent pair of I-cord rims together along the "X". Finally, loosely sew ends of each pair of I-cord rims to rim or handle, so surface is continuous. Weave in all ends. Felt according to general instructions on pages 16-19, fine tune the shape, and set out to dry. After felting, you may find it useful to sew the compartments together near the base for stability.

Please read this section before going on

This two-page spread is bound to amuse you *as well as* confuse you unless you make a paper Moebius model like you did in the introductory chapter, then slice it in thirds lengthwise, as if it were a three-lane road and you are cutting down the yellow lines. Once you recover from your astonishment, continue reading to learn how *to*, and how *not to*, knit one.

The original design, pictured above, was not supposed to look like this, but was to replicate the clever trick you just performed with the paper model. Delirious with Moebius-inspired delusional hubris, I'd unknowingly embarked on this adventure with three, rather than one, crossings in the MCO, which meant that my result did not resemble your model, but its extremely loopy relative pictured above. I nearly tossed out the miserable thing, but after much cajoling by knitters and non-knitters alike, who declared the mutant mesmerizing, I'm dutifully offering it to you, with instructions for making it as a mishap (as above) or correctly (see Miss-Te and Callie on the next page).

MESMERIZING HALF-MOEBIUS MISHAP

The inner scarf can be distinguished by its arrowheads, and the outer scarf by its diagonals, though they were both born with arrowheads. The outer scarf, poor thing, has become two-edged and two-sided, with one ivory edge and a contrast edge. The inner scarf remains true Moebius, with one continuous (contrast) edge.

Yarn: 200 yds main color, 75 yds contrast color
Needles: suitable size circular 47"– 55" length, second long circular needle of similar or smaller size (to be used as a very long stitch holder)
Notions: tapestry needle, stitch markers
Gauge: this is up to you, oh adventurous knitter!
Finished size: too convoluted to measure
Stitch guide: See page 112 for abbreviations, page 109 for waste yarn, and page 110 for I-cord.

Begin with an extra crossing in the MCO

With main color, MCO 86, with *three* crossings (see page 96 for instructions and illustration). Place marker.

Begin diagonal pattern

Rounds 1-2: *Knit 2, p2, repeat from *.
Rounds 3-4: Purl 1, *k2, p2, repeat from *, end p1. Rounds 5-6: *Purl 2, k2, repeat from *.
Rounds 7-8: Knit 1, *p2, k2, repeat from *, end k1. Repeat rounds 1-8 once. Cut tail of yarn. *With waste yarn*, k 1 round. With main color, repeat rounds 1-8 once.

Edgings

Loosely bind off entire edge with main color. Pick up all sts along *inner* scarf's waste yarn edge. With second circular needle, pick up all sts along *outer* scarf's waste yarn edge. Snip and unravel the waste yarn to separate the 2 scarves' edges (scarves will remain entwined). Secure stitches on second needle holding *outer* scarf by knotting thick rubber bands around needle tips. With contrast color, k 4 rounds on *inner* scarf's edge and loosely bind off. Use same needle and contrast color to knit *outer* scarf's stitches from second needle, then set aside second needle. Knit 3 rounds, and loosely bind off. Weave in all ends.

Commentary

You cannot untangle this thing, because it has so many twists, resulting from the extra crossings given the original scarf during the MCO. That extra twist multiplied into what I think may be six full twists in the outer scarf. It loops around the inner scarf three times! Lest you think I am cuckoo for having included this strange pattern, let me point out that it can be worn as a Celtic sort of scarf and will actually create the illusion of an ample bust, should that be something you have been desiring all your life. It also provides one of several answers to the question, what *does* happen if you have too many crossings?

MESMERIZING HALF-MOEBIUS MARVEL

MODELED BY A MARVELOUS MARE

Miss-Te, with her best friend Callie Bartlett, is modeling a Moebius horse lead, a correctly knit version of the original design. If your horse loves you as much as Miss-Te loves Callie, a gentle Moebius horse lead is all you need!

MCO 100 (check for *one* crossing!) and k 10 rounds. Using fishing line (of a knittable gauge) as waste yarn, k 3 rounds, then k 20 rounds with regular yarn. Bind off. Now you can felt your Moebius Horse-Lead in one piece, and afterwards remove the fishing line, which will not stick at all to the un-bound-off felted edges, leaving them stable. I knit mine with 2 skeins of Cascade Pastaza, a wonderful llama-wool blend, at a gauge of 12 sts = 4" (10 cm), on size 13 needles. Felt according to general instructions on pages 16-19. It is likely to shrink little in length, but about 35% in width. The finished mesmerizing marvel will resemble your paper model from the other page.

I've truly never seen him in such deep bliss.
- woman watching her cat melting into a Moebius bed

Chapter Eight - Feline Bliss Beds

*I*t never even occurred to me in the early days of writing the first *Treasury of Magical Knitting* to knit a cat bed. I was so enamored of the different species of Moebius scarves that grazed in the pastures of my imagination that it was months before I even noticed the Moebius-collared capes and Moebius-banded hats on the far horizon. They joined us, and one day a friendly Moebius-banded hat rolled over to reveal there was such a thing as a Moebius-banded bowl. No sooner had I made the bowl and filled it with yarn, than it became obvious that a larger version would make a divine nest for a cat. And as you can see from the photos, this is so. Just wait until your cat tiptoes into one of these beds, melts into the warm curves, and begins to purr. The cats in my home have the luxury of wandering among seven different beds, and it is a beautiful sight to see.

Steps of knitting a Feline Bliss Bed

- Knit a large Moebius band and finish it with applied I-cord.

- Pick up stitches at the base of the band and knit a large bowl.

- Felt the bed.

- Block, dry, and invite your cat to enter her new sanctuary.

Fitting a bed to your cat

In this book you'll find six feline bliss beds to choose from, ranging from nineteen to twelve inches in diameter. I've watched big cats try to climb into a bed that seemed decidedly too small, settling in and oozing over the side like a soft serve ice cream cone about to go south, purring with pleasure. Come back a few minutes later, and they've somehow wiggled down into a joyful fetal position, fitting perfectly.

The cats in my home love to hop from bed to bed. As you can see on the following page, tiny Mishka (about five pounds) is happy in the Red Rose Bed, although it could hold two or three of her. When she went on her way, her companion Toby (about eighteen pounds) took her place, purring as he overflowed the edges of the same bed.

I suggest you sneak up on your sleeping cat with a tape measure in hand. Measure the angelic creature's average width and make the bed a little bigger, or a lot bigger. During the felting and blocking process, you can adjust the size simply by felting for a longer or shorter time.

Yarn choice

You must use a yarn which will felt to a sturdy, thick fabric, like those I have chosen. Cascade Pastaza or Chuckanut Bay Perendale are also excellent choices. If you use a lighter yarn, try using two strands held together.

Felting & blocking

Follow the felting instructions on pages 16-19, leaving the bed to agitate as long as necessary for it to thicken and shrink. If the sides and bottom are uneven when you take it out of the washing machine, then push and stretch it until smooth and shapely, perhaps standing in the center to hold the base flat, while pulling the sides up. To finish it off, try my secret cat bed blocking device: a wheel barrow inner tube! Until knitting shops start to stock this unusual knitting accessory, you'll have to go to a hardware store, where they cost about eight dollars. Just insert the inner tube in the bed and drive to the nearest service station, and grin like a Cheshire Cat if other motorists stare while you blow up your cat bed, checking the inflation with a tape measure instead of a tire gauge. Leave the inner tube in the bed until it is dry, then deflate it, put it away for the next bed, and call your cat.

RED ROSE BED

This is your basic cat bed, which you may dress up with a contrast color rim or I-cord, embellishments from page 25, or felted fringe. The rim is narrower than the belly, so your cat can sink his slinky self against the sides and bliss out in the snug embrace of thick soft wool. To my surprise, I've noticed that cats still like to sleep in these beds on very hot summer days, even with the sun falling across them through the window! Petite Burmese Mishka, to the right, divides her nap time among the large beds in this chapter, and the small one which was made just for her, in Chapter Six. Her Maine Coon companion Toby, below, luxuriously fills the same bed to overflowing.

Yarn: Crystal Palace Iceland (100% wool, 100 g/109 yds, 6 wpi) cherry red, 6 balls.

Needles: (you may require a different size to get correct gauge) size 13 (9 mm) circular, 47" - 60" length, also 16" length

Notions: tapestry needle, stitch marker, wheel barrow inner tube recommended

Gauge: (before felting) 12 sts = 4" (10 cm)

Finished Size: Before felting, base diameter 27", band circumference 64". After felting, base diameter 17", band circumference 50".

Stitch Guide: See page 112 for abbreviations, pages 110 - 111 for applied I-cord, page 109 for waste yarn and knitting with two circular needles, and page 108 for turning a Moebius band into a simple circle.

Begin with rim

MCO 200. Place marker. *Knit 1 round. Purl 1 round. Repeat from * 3 times. Finish edge with applied I-cord, and graft or weave ends together.

Sides

Pick up and knit 200 sts directly beneath I-cord edge, 1 st for each I-cord st. This will bring you halfway around the edge of the rim, so that you can bring the two needle tips together to join and knit in the round, without any twist on the needle. The half-twist that makes the rim a Moebius hangs beneath the stitches on your needle. Place marker and k 4 rounds.

Increase

*Knit 2, k1f&b, repeat from * to marker, ending k2. (266 sts) Knit 10 rounds.

Decrease for bottom

Switch to two circular needles once you have too few sts to easily fit around the 16" needle. *Knit 14, k2tog, repeat from *, end k10. (250 sts) *Knit 8, k2tog, repeat from *. (225 sts) Knit 4 rounds. *Knit 8, k2tog, repeat from *, end k5. (203 sts) Knit 4 rounds. *Knit 8, k2tog, repeat from *, end k3. (183 sts) Knit 4 rounds. *Knit 7, k2tog, repeat from *, end k3. (163 sts) Knit 4 rounds. *Knit 7, k2tog, repeat from *, end k1. (145 sts) Knit 4 rounds. *Knit 7, k2tog, repeat from *, end k1. (129 sts) Knit 4 rounds. *Knit 7, k2tog, repeat from *, end k3. (115 sts) Knit 2 rounds. *Knit 7, k2tog, repeat from *, end k7. (103 sts) Knit 2 rounds. *Knit 6, k2tog, repeat from *, end k7. (91 sts) Knit 2 rounds. *Knit 6, k2tog, repeat from *, end k3. (80 sts) Knit 2 rounds. *Knit 6, k2tog, repeat from *. (70 sts) Knit 2 rounds. *Knit 5, k2tog, repeat from *. (60 sts) Knit 2 rounds. *Knit 4, k2tog, repeat from *. (50 sts)

Knit 2 rounds. *Knit 3, k2tog, repeat from *. (40 sts) Knit 1 round. *Knit 2, k2tog, repeat from *. (30 sts) Knit 1 round. *Knit 1, k2tog, repeat from *. (20 sts) *Knit 2tog, repeat from *. (10 sts) Cut tail, thread through remaining sts, pull snug, and weave in securely.

Felting

Felt according to general instructions on pages 16-19. See page 81 for special tips on felting and blocking cat beds. Don't forget your wheelbarrow inner tube!

Rainforest Nest

Toby has quite a few choices for nap time, and here he has chosen the Rainforest Nest. You'll find the nest's cousin, the Mossy Moebius Basket, in Chapter Two. It was the Mossy Moebius Basket that inspired me to attempt a cat-sized basket. I envisioned a mossy handle arching over the sleeping cat, and how nice it might be to drape a cloth over the handle to give the cat a secluded hide-away. But it didn't work out. No matter how intensively I felted the bed, the handle just refused to stand up. I briefly considered inserting wire, or some other kind of support, but finally abandoned the idea and eliminated the handle. This also made the bed a non-Moebius, but I suspect some of you will be grateful for the simplicity of the pattern.

Yarn: Crystal Palace Labrador (100% wool, 90 yds /100 g, 6.5 wpi) Green Forest Combo, 8 balls; Crystal Palace Fizz (100% polyester, 120 yds/ 50 g, 15 wpi) Sage Mix, 6 balls; 1 yard waste yarn.

Needles: (you may require a different size to get correct gauge) size 13 (9 mm) circular, 32" - 47" length, also second circular (16" is ideal; see "begin with I-cord rim" on next page) or 2 double-pointed needles.

Notions: tapestry needle, marker, wheel barrow inner tube recommended

Gauge: (before felting) 10 sts = 4" (10 cm) using one strand of Labrador held together with one strand of Fizz.

Finished size: Before felting, base diameter 30", sides 6" high. After felting, 20" and 4".

Stitch Guide: See page 112 for abbreviations, page 110 - 111 for applied I-cord, page 109 for waste yarn and knitting with two circular needles, and page 108 for turning a Moebius band into a simple circle. *Knit with one strand of Fizz and one strand of Labrador held together throughout.*

Begin with I-cord rim

Cast on 3 sts. *Knit 3, replace all 3 sts on left needle, repeat from * 179 times. (180 rounds total) If you do this on two double-pointed needles or one short circular, you don't even have to replace the 3 sts back on the left needle. Instead, just slide the sts to the bottom of the needle that just knit them, and use the other needle (in the case of a short circular, the other end of the circular) to knit the next round. Once you complete a long rope of 180 rounds, bind off and sew the ends together.

Pick up and begin sides

Use your long circular needle to pick up 180 sts along the edge of the I-cord circle. Place marker and k 2 rounds. *Knit 2, k1f&b, repeat from *. (240 sts) *Knit 23, k1f&b, repeat from *. (250 sts) Knit 18 rounds, or more, if you'd like taller sides.

Decrease for bottom

*Knit 8, k2tog, repeat from *. (225 sts) Knit 4 rounds. *Knit 8, k2tog, repeat from *, end k5. (203 sts) Knit 4 rounds. *Knit 8, k2tog, repeat from *, end k3. (183 sts) Knit 4 rounds. *Knit 7, k2tog, repeat from *, end k3. (163 sts) Knit 4 rounds. *Knit 7, k2tog, repeat from *, end k1. (145 sts) Knit 4 rounds. *Knit 7, k2tog, repeat from *, end k1. (129 sts) Knit 4 rounds. *Knit 7, k2tog, repeat from *, end k3. (115 sts) Knit 2 rounds. *Knit 7, k2tog, repeat from *, end k7. (103 sts) Knit 2 rounds. *Knit 6, k2tog, repeat from *, end k7. (91 sts) Knit 2 rounds. *Knit 6, k2tog, repeat from *, end k3. (80 sts) Knit 2 rounds. *Knit 6, k2tog, repeat from *. (70 sts) Knit 2 rounds. *Knit 5, k2tog, repeat from *. (60 sts) Knit 2 rounds. *Knit 4, k2tog, repeat from *. (50 sts) Knit 2 rounds. *Knit 3, k2tog, repeat from *. (40 sts) Knit 2 rounds. *Knit 2, k2tog, repeat from *. (30 sts) Knit 1 round. *Knit 1, k2tog, repeat from *. (20 sts) *Knit 2tog, repeat from *. (10 sts) Cut tail, thread end through remaining sts, pull snug, and weave in securely. Weave in all ends.

Felting

Felt according to general instructions on pages 16-19. See page 81 for special tips on felting and blocking cat beds.

FRINGED FOREST BED

Felted fringe dances around this cat bed with wild abandon, matching your cat's spirit and fluffy tail. You'll find a similar, much smaller version in Chapter Six, with petite Mishka nestled inside. And if you don't have a cat in your home just now, the bed makes a splendid large yarn basket. Toby, above, began his nap by laying half in and half out of the bed, then migrated inside, leaving squashed edges to tell the tale.

Yarn: Crystal Palace Iceland (100% wool, 100 g/109 yds, 6 wpi) forest green, 7 balls.

Needles: (you may require a different size to get correct gauge) size 11 (9 mm) circular, 55" - 60" length, also 16" length

Notions: tapestry needle, stitch markers, wheel barrow inner tube recommended

Gauge: (before felting)
14 sts = 4" (10 cm)

Finished size: Before felting, base diameter 27", band circumference 66". After felting, base 17", band 50".

Stitch Guide: See page 112 for abbreviations, pages 110 - 111 for applied I-cord, page 109 for waste yarn and knitting with two circular needles, page 108 for turning a Moebius band into a simple circle, and page 68 for fringe.

Begin with rim
MCO 190. Place marker. *Knit 1 round. Purl 1 round. Repeat from * twice. Finish edge with applied I-cord. Weave ends together.

Sides
Pick up and knit 190 sts directly beneath I-cord edge, 1 st for each I-cord st. This will bring you halfway around the edge of the rim, so that you can bring the two needle tips together to join and knit in the round, without any twist on the needle. The half-twist that makes the rim a Moebius hangs beneath the stitches on your needle. Place marker and k 3 rounds.

Increase
*Knit 2, k1f&b, repeat from *, ending k1. (253 sts) Knit 10 rounds. Decrease away 3 sts in the next round. (250 sts)

Decrease for bottom

Switch to two circular needles once you have too few sts to easily fit around the 16" needle. *Knit 14, k2tog, repeat from *, end k10. (250 sts) *Knit 8, k2tog, repeat from *. (225 sts) Knit 4 rounds. *Knit 8, k2tog, repeat from *, end k5. (203 sts) Knit 4 rounds. *Knit 8, k2tog, repeat from *, end k3. (183 sts) Knit 4 rounds. *Knit 7, k2tog, repeat from *, end k3. (163 sts) Knit 4 rounds. *Knit 7, k2tog, repeat from *, end k1. (145 sts) Knit 4 rounds. *Knit 7, k2tog, repeat from *, end k1. (129 sts) Knit 4 rounds. *Knit 7, k2tog, repeat from *, end k3. (115 sts) Knit 2 rounds. *Knit 7, k2tog, repeat from *, end k7. (103 sts) Knit 2 rounds. *Knit 6, k2tog, repeat from *, end k7. (91 sts) Knit 2 rounds. *Knit 6, k2tog, repeat from *, end k3. (80 sts) Knit 2 rounds. *Knit 6, k2tog, repeat from *. (70 sts) Knit 2 rounds. *Knit 5, k2tog, repeat from *. (60 sts) Knit 2 rounds. *Knit 4, k2tog, repeat from *. (50 sts) Knit 2 rounds. *Knit 3, k2tog, repeat from *. (40 sts) Knit 2 rounds. *Knit 2, k2tog, repeat from *. (30 sts) Knit 1 round. *Knit 1, k2tog, repeat from *. (20 sts) *Knit 2tog, repeat from *. (10 sts) Cut tail, thread end through remaining sts, pull snug, and weave in securely.

Fringe

Cut approximately 95 eleven inch lengths of yarn and attach them every other st immediately below the lower I-cord rim.

Felting

Felt according to general instructions on pages 16-19. See page 81 for special tips on felting and blocking cat beds. To keep the fringe from matting together too much, you will have to pull it out of the wash every few minutes for the first half or so of felting and pull the strands apart. After a while you will find that the fringe no longer seems to mat much more.

Yarn and design suggestions

All the cat beds require good sturdy felting yarns, so check out your substitution choices by making one of the wallets or needle cozies in Chapter One. If you'd like the bed to be taller, just knit more rounds in between the increase round and the beginning of the decrease rounds.

Paws & Tail Cat Bed

A vision of this cat bed came to me in the wee hours, making me smile. The bed itself is a cat, who holds your cat. And if you put a bit of catnip down one of the hollow paws (you can see an opening in the photo) your darling will have a game to play when she wakes up from her womb-like nap. Mishka, whom you see here, is a petite Burmese, taking up only half the bed. She is about half the size of the average cat, so you can imagine what your own cat might look like in this bed.

Yarn: Crystal Palace Iceland (100% wool, 100 g/109 yds, 6 wpi) cream, 8 balls.

Needles: (you may require a different size to get correct gauge) size 13 (9 mm) circular, 55" - 60" length, also 16" length

Notions: tapestry needle, stitch markers, wheel barrow inner tube recommended

Gauge: (before felting) 12 sts = 4" (10 cm)

Finished Size: Before felting: base diameter 30", band circumference 70", rim to center bottom 27", legs 12", tail 21". After felting: base 21", band 48", rim to center bottom 15", legs 8", tail 14".

Stitch Guide: See page 112 for abbreviations, pages 110 - 111 for applied I-cord, page 109 for waste yarn and knitting with two circular needles, page 108 for turning a Moebius band into a simple circle.

Begin with rim

MCO 190, and place marker on right needle tip. *Knit 1 round. Purl 1 round. Repeat from * 3 times. Finish edge with applied I-cord. Weave ends together.

Sides

Pick up and knit 190 sts directly beneath I-cord edge, 1 st for each I-cord st. This will bring you halfway around the edge of the rim, so that you can bring the two needle tips together to join and knit in the round, without any twist on the needle. The half-twist that makes the rim a Moebius hangs beneath the stitches on your needle. Place marker and k 5 rounds.

Increase

*Knit 2, k1f&b, repeat from * to marker, ending k1. (253 sts) Knit 18 rounds. Decrease 3 sts during the next round. (250 sts)

Decrease, and create openings

Switch to two circular needles once you have too few sts to fit around the 16" needle. *Knit 8, k2tog, repeat from * to marker, end k3. (225 sts) Knit 4 rounds. *Knit 8, k2tog, repeat from * to marker, end k5. (203 sts). Knit 1 round. In next round, work waste yarn sections for legs and tail as follows: k30, work 10-st waste yarn section, k20, work 10-st waste yarn section, k76, work 10-st waste yarn section, k47. Knit 2 rounds. *Knit 8, k2tog, repeat from *, end k3. (183 sts) Knit 4 rounds. *Knit 7, k2tog, repeat from *, end k3. (163 sts) Knit 4 rounds. *Knit 7, k2tog, repeat from *, end k1. (145 sts) Knit 4 rounds. *Knit 7, k2tog, repeat from *, end k1. (129 sts) Knit 4 rounds. *Knit 7, k2tog, repeat from *, end k3. (115 sts) Knit 2 rounds. *Knit 7, k2tog, repeat from *, end k7. (103 sts) Knit 2 rounds. *Knit 6, k2tog, repeat from *, end k7. (91 sts) Knit 2 rounds. *Knit 6, k2tog, repeat from *, end k3. (80 sts) Knit 2 rounds. *Knit 6, k2tog, repeat from *. (70 sts) Knit 2 rounds. *Knit 5, k2tog, repeat from *. (60 sts) Knit 2 rounds. *Knit 4, k2tog, repeat from *. (50 sts) Knit 2 rounds. *Knit 3, k2tog, repeat from *. (40 sts) Knit 2 rounds. *Knit 2, k2tog, repeat from *. (30 sts) Knit 1 round. *Knit 1, k2tog, repeat from *. (20 sts) *Knit 2tog, repeat from *. (10 sts) Cut tail, thread end through remaining sts, pull snug, and weave in securely.

Legs

With 2 circular needles, work a leg in each front waste yarn section by picking up 20, plus 2 in each corner. (24 sts) Knit until 9" long. Knit 13, k2tog, k2, k2tog, k2, k2tog, k1. (21 sts) K 1 round. K12, *k1f&b, k1, repeat from * 4 times, end k1f&b. (26 sts) Knit 6 rounds. K2tog, k10, ssk, k2tog, k8, ssk. (22 sts) Knit 2tog, k8, ssk, k10. (20 sts) Graft the 10 sts left on each needle together, or bind off and sew closed.

Tail

Pick up 20 sts in remaining opening plus 2 in each corner. (24 sts) Knit until 14" long. *Knit 4, k2tog, repeat from * 3 times. (20 sts) Knit 1". *Knit 2, k2tog, repeat from * 4 times. (15 sts) Knit 1". *Knit 1, k2tog, repeat from * 4 times (10 sts). K 3 rounds. *Knit 2tog, repeat from * 4 times. (5 sts) Knit 1 round, k2tog twice, k1, cut yarn, thread through remaining 3 sts, and weave in ends.

Felting

Felt according to general instructions on pages 16-19. See page 81 for special tips on felting and blocking cat beds. Poke the end of a wooden spoon inside the legs and tail every two minutes for the first ten minutes of felting, so they remain open.

Yarn and design suggestions

Some white yarns do not felt well, so if you substitute, felt a swatch first, perhaps by making a needle cozy. And if you'd like to add paws and a tail to any of the other beds or bowls or baskets in this book, try Elizabeth Zimmermann's after-thought pocket technique: before felting, decide where each appendage should grow, snip the middle stitch, and unravel sideways, picking up the required number of stitches on a pair of circular needles. You could, of course, add rear legs as well. I don't know what stopped me.

Fair Isle Nest

This unfelted Fair Isle nest is knit with a double strand of yarn, and supported by a felted liner, so it is especially warm and snug. Paw prints circle the sides, and the band is thick with bumpy moss stitch. Handsome Shey, whom you see here, is a moss aficionado and apparent pacifist who returns from nocturnal adventures with mouse-sized clumps of moss, which he proudly leaves for his owners in the hallway. He feels right at home wrapped in moss stitch. See how he rests his paw right on the mossy Moebius twist?

Yarn: Philosopher's 2-Ply Wool (100% wool, 4 oz/ 275 yds, 11 wpi), 2 skeins dark purple, 1 skein each pale blue, pale green, light purple, dark blue, and plum. *See liner pattern on page 92 for liner yarn and needle requirements.*

Needles: (you may require a different size to get correct gauge) size 7 (4.5 mm) circular, 47 - 60" length, also 36" length; size 9 (5.5 mm) circular, 36" length.

Notions: tapestry needle, stitch markers, wheel barrow inner tube recommended

Gauge: (double strand of yarn) 14 sts = 4" (10 cm) on smaller needle

Finished Size: Circumference 54", base diameter 17", height 6".

Stitch Guide: See page 112 for abbreviations, page 110 - 111 for applied I-cord, page 109 for waste yarn and knitting with two circular needles, and page 108 for turning a Moebius band into a simple circle. *Knit with two strands of yarn throughout.*

Begin with rim

With double strand of dark purple and longer size 7 needle, MCO 138. Place marker. Knit 2, p2 to marker, repeat round once. Purl 2, k2 to marker, repeat round once. Repeat last 4 rounds twice. Knit 2, p2 to marker, repeat round once. Finish edge with applied I-cord. Weave ends together.

Sides

With 36" size 7 needle, pick up and knit 138 sts directly beneath I-cord edge, 1 st for each I-cord st. This will bring you halfway around the edge of the rim, so that you can bring the two needle tips together to join and knit in the round, without any twist on the needle. The half-twist that makes the rim a Moebius hangs beneath the stitches on your needle. Place marker and k 2 rounds.

Increase

*Knit 2, k1f&b, repeat from * to marker. (184 sts) Knit 1 round. *Knit 22, k1f&b, repeat from *. (192 sts) Knit 1 round. *Switch to larger needle* and begin Fair Isle Cat Paw design from chart. When design is complete, *switch back to smaller needle* and continue with dark purple. *Knit 10, k2tog, repeat from * to marker. (176 sts)

Decrease for bottom

When there are too few stitches to go around the 36" needle, use 2 circular needles, or use a shorter circular needle until there are too few stitches for that too.
*Knit 9, k2tog, repeat from * to marker. Knit 1 round. (160 sts) *Knit 8, k2tog, repeat from * to marker. Knit 1 round. (144 sts) *Knit 7, k2tog, repeat from * to marker. Knit 1 round. (128 sts) *Knit 6, k2tog, repeat from * to marker. Knit 1 round. (112 sts) *Knit 5, k2tog, repeat from * to marker. Knit 1 round. (96 sts) *Knit 10, k2tog, repeat from * to marker. Knit 1 round. (88 sts) *Knit 9, k2tog, repeat from * to marker. Knit 1 round. (80 sts) *Knit 8, k2tog, repeat from * to marker. Knit 1 round. (72 sts) *Knit 7, k2tog, repeat from * to marker. Knit 1 round. (64 sts) *Knit 6, k2tog, repeat from * to marker. Knit 1 round. (56 sts) *Knit 5, k2tog, repeat from * to marker. Knit 1 round. (48 sts) *Knit 4, k2tog, repeat from * to marker. Knit 1 round. (40 sts) *Knit 3, k2tog, repeat from * to marker. Knit 1 round. (32 sts) *Knit 2, k2tog, repeat from * to marker. Knit 1 round. (24 sts) *Knit 1, k2tog, repeat from * to marker. Knit 1 round. (16 sts) *Knit 2tog, repeat from * to marker. (8 sts) Cut tail of yarn and thread through remaining 8 sts, then weave in ends.

Finishing

Wash and spin dry, then block the bed by inflating a wheel barrow inner tube inside it, inflated to a 54" diameter. Pull the sides up above the inner tube, stretching the bottom until it flattens. While you're waiting for it to dry, start the felted liner (see following page).

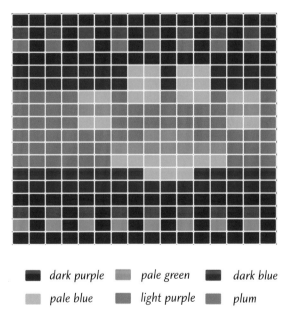

| ![dark purple] dark purple | ![pale green] pale green | ![dark blue] dark blue |
| ![pale blue] pale blue | ![light purple] light purple | ![plum] plum |

The Fair Isle Cat Paw design is a 16-stitch repeat over 18 rounds.

Liner for Fair Isle Nest

You can see that the inside of the bed is plain instead of textured and colorful. This heavy felted liner is necessary to give body to the softer outer bed. Mooshie was the first kitty to test out this bed, and gave it a five-paw rating. You may find it helpful to stitch the outer bed to the inner bed along the rim. And since Philosopher's Wool felts little or not at all, you can launder both inner and outer beds together without fear of the outer bed shrinking. You may also use this pattern as a stand-alone bed if you wish, perhaps adding your own designs (see embellishment instructions page 25). It is similar in size to the Red Rose Bed, but with a smaller opening and somewhat taller sides.

Yarn: Crystal Palace Yarns Iceland (100% wool, 100 g/109 yds, 6 wpi) purple, 6 balls.

Needles: (you may require a different size to get correct gauge) size 13 (9 mm) circular, 55" - 60" length, also 16" length

Notions: tapestry needle, stitch markers, safety pins, wheel barrow inner tube recommended

Gauge: (before felting) 12 sts = 4" (10 cm)

Finished Size: Before felting, base diameter 27", height 9". After felting, 17", height 6".

Stitch Guide: See page 112 for abbreviations, page 110 - 111 for applied I-cord, page 109 for waste yarn and knitting with two circular needles, and page 108 for turning a Moebius band into a simple circle.

Begin with rim

MCO 175. Place marker. *Knit 1 round. Purl 1 round. Repeat from * 3 times. Finish edge by working applied I-cord on first 175 sts, placing safety pins along the edge every 10" or so to identify this half. Make sure to mark the beginning and the end of the 175 sts with safety pins as well. Continue towards marker as follows: *work 5 rounds *(a round is each cycle of k2, k2tog, replace all 3 sts on left needle)* of applied I-cord, then 1 decrease round: k2, k3tog, replace all 3 sts on left needle. Repeat from * until all sts are bound off. Weave ends together. *The half with decreases becomes the upper rim, and tips inwards. The half marked with safety pins becomes the lower, wider rim.*

Sides

Pick up and k 175 sts directly beneath the I-cord edge which is marked with safety pins (where you worked normal applied I-cord), 1 st for each I-cord st. This will bring you halfway around the edge of the rim, so that you can bring the two needle tips together to join and knit in the round, without any twist on the needle. The half-twist that makes the rim a Moebius hangs beneath the stitches on your needle. Place marker and k 4 rounds. *Knit 1, k1f&b, repeat from *, ending k1. (262 sts) Knit 15 rounds.

Decrease for bottom

Switch to two circular needles once you have too few sts to easily fit around the 16" needle. *Knit 19, k2tog, repeat from *, end k10. (250 sts) *Knit 8, k2tog, repeat from *. (225 sts) Knit 4 rounds. *Knit 8, k2tog, repeat from *, end k5. (203 sts) Knit 4 rounds. *Knit 8, k2tog, repeat from *, end k3. (183 sts) Knit 4 rounds. *Knit 7, k2tog, repeat from *, end k3. (163 sts) Knit 4 rounds. *Knit 7, k2tog, repeat from *, end k1. (145 sts) Knit 4 rounds. *Knit 7, k2tog, repeat from *, end k1. (129 sts) Knit 4 rounds. *Knit 7, k2tog, repeat from *, end k3. (115 sts) Knit 2 rounds.

*Knit 7, k2tog, repeat from *, end k7. (103 sts) Knit 2 rounds. *Knit 6, k2tog, repeat from *, end k7. (91 sts) Knit 2 rounds. *Knit 6, k2tog, repeat from *, end k3. (80 sts) Knit 2 rounds. *Knit 6, k2tog, repeat from *. (70 sts) Knit 2 rounds. *Knit 5, k2tog, repeat from *. (60 sts) Knit 2 rounds. *Knit 4, k2tog, repeat from *. (50 sts) Knit 2 rounds. *Knit 3, k2tog, repeat from *. (40 sts) Knit 2 rounds. *Knit 2, k2tog, repeat from *. (30 sts) Knit 1 round. *Knit 1, k2tog, repeat from *. (20 sts) *Knit 2tog, repeat from *. (10 sts) Cut tail, thread through remaining sts, pull snug, and weave in securely.

Felting

Felt according to general instructions on pages 16-19. See page 81 for special tips on felting and blocking cat beds. If you use the wheelbarrow inner tube method, inflate the inner tube to the same diameter for the liner as you did for the outer bed. If you've already finished the outer bed, you may pull it over the liner and block them together. This is ideal.

CHAPTER NINE - THE TRIFOLD SERIES

Just weeks before this book was to be sent off to the printer, the Moebius Trifold spirits breezed into my home and called out, "Wait! You haven't seen *us* yet!" And my love affair with the Moebius gathered fresh momentum.

If you love working with your hands (and of course you do, for you are a knitter), you'll find the process of coaxing shapes from the freshly felted trifolds to be kindred to working with clay sculpture. I discovered by chance that the rim of a Somersaulting Rim Trifold Bowl could be spread and pulled and patted into the flowing curves and swells you see on this page. You can pull upwards on the "petals" and massage the wall below into a swell, then press down on the concave curves in between. Or, simply blow up a balloon inside the Somersaulting Rim Trifold Bowl, leaving the rim as a round flat band above a beautiful deep bowl. Perhaps you will discover other ways of manipulating the pliant, freshly felted material.

The rings in the bottom of the bowl were happenstance as well – I was running out of black yarn so had to use some white! In case you wonder where designers get their ideas, it's often from circumstances just like this - making do with what one has at hand, and of course, being ever eager to explore the surprises hidden in that fine recyclable material known as mistakes.

One of my favorite Moebius scarves in the first *Treasury of Magical Knitting* is the Sandstone and Sky Scarf, which was lightly felted and so sensual that I kept dreaming of making something more with this wonderful yarn, which felts into the softest, most pliant fabric you can imagine. When the trifold bug got me, I realized that the felted stripes I'd used in the scarf would really highlight the geometry of a Trifold. It was one of those leap-out-of-bed-in-the-middle-of-the-night moments.

Unlike most felted designs, the Trifold Sandstone and Sky Bag requires almost no shaping after felting. This is partly the result of the very cooperative yarn, and partly the result of the design itself, whose geometry seems to organize the felt to match its framework. As you knit the bag with its three folds and then its three-sided pyramid bowl, you may wonder if sorting things into threes contains an enchantment of some kind, for the knitting, and seeing the stripes reveal the geometry, brings an inexplicable sense of comfort and glee. And it looks great worn with the scarf!

The Trifold Knitter's Bowl, with its six pouches and petal-covered inner bowl for yarn, has taken over the small table beside my knitting chair. I put a small lazy Susan underneath it, so it spins around to give me every tool I need. Your yarn won't roll away or get dusty if you put it inside this bowl, pulling the strand from between the overlapping petals. And your cat won't be able to chase it, although it is true that if your cat is small, you may find him hiding inside the bowl with your yarn if you're not careful!

The bowl takes longer to knit than most of the pieces in this book, but I think you'll find it well worth the time. There is something endearing about making all the little woolly cubbyholes, and the three petals that close the top, yet leave it so easy to open, are enchanting. Everything is in three's – three petals, three half-twists, and six (twice three!) pouches.

TRIFOLD MOEBIUS MAGIC

A Trifold Moebius requires not one, but *three* crossings in the initial MCO set-up. Remember the train that leaves a single crossing of the right needle and the cable, then runs along parallel tracks all the way to the left needle, as shown on page twelve? Well, our trifold train leaves an initial crossing of cable and cable, then runs into two additional crossings. You will count three crossings of *cable and cable*, as shown in the picture to the right (yarn is tied around each crossing).

Start with one crossing of cable and cable near the right needle, then rotate the left needle around the cable one full rotation. This will give you a total of three crossings, with cables parallel in between. *(One full rotation actually produces two crossings. You start with one crossing, then add one full rotation, making three crossings.)* Begin with your right needle parallel to the cable, and isolate the first crossing by tying a bit of yarn around the "X" the cables make, tying the yarn from side to side in between the cables to secure the crossing so it won't try and sneak away. Move down to a second crossing, and secure it as well. Find the third, and secure it. The needles will cross one another, but this is irrelevant. If you still have extra crossings after securing the three you need, rotate them away by rotating the left needle around the cable.

Once you've established your three crossings (you can untie the yarn now), everything proceeds as normal, except that you'll have to maneuver the knitting around the needles a little more because of the twists.

After you have knit a number of rounds, your knitting will take the shape you see below. Do you recognize the recycling symbol? There are actually two commonly used versions of the recycling symbol, both of them Moebii, which appear so similar that few notice the difference. But one is a single fold Moebius, and the other trifold. We've been surrounded by Moebii all along!

A trifold Moebius underway

One is a mirror reflection of the other. Your trifold may look like either one; it doesn't make any difference.

In a trifold pattern, you will pick up stitches from the rim in a certain way. You will be instructed to pick up a certain number of stitches at each of the three diagonal folds, and a certain number of stitches along the I-cord border in between the diagonal folds.

You may pick up the I-cord stitches either along the outer edge of the I-cord, or along the purl bumps directly beside the I-cord.

If you pick up stitches along the outer edge of the I-cord, your felted piece will have a relatively smooth transition between rim and bowl.

If you pick up stitches in the purl bumps beside the I-cord, the I-cord will stand above the felted surface.

You may have noticed that I am using a Denise interchangeable needle to pick up the stitches, and that one tip is smaller than the other. The smaller tip makes it especially easy to pick up stitches, and can be exchanged for the larger tip when you begin knitting. But don't change it without first noticing how using a smaller *left* needle and a correct size *right* needle facilitates the flow of your stitches along the left needle. This little trick will not change your gauge, because only the right needle determines gauge. I use this method all the time.

SOMERSAULTING RIM TRIFOLD BOWL

The rim of this Trifold Bowl somersaults along a never-ending Moebius path, a vision of perfect harmony. The bowl is scarcely any more difficult to knit than its simpler cousins. If there had been more pages in the book, I would have added a tall Trifold bowl, one with five twists (it has to be an odd number, or it's not a Moebius), and who knows what else, but I ran out of time and space. But you can bet that by the time you read this I'll have knit them anyway.

Yarn: Chuckanut Bay Yarns 14 ply (100% Perendale wool, 200 g/ 220 yds, 7 wpi), black (main color) and (contrast color) white, 1 skein each; *or* work with 2 strands held together of Cascade 220 (100% wool, 100 g/ 220 yds, 11 wpi), 2 skeins tomato (main color), and 1 skein indigo (contrast color)

Needles: (you may require a different size to get correct gauge) size 13 (9 mm) circular, 47" – 60" length, also 16 - 24" length

Notions: tapestry needle, stitch markers, and a small sturdy dinner plate for blocking

Gauge: (before felting) 9 sts = 4" (10 cm) If using Cascade 220, check gauge with 2 strands of yarn held together.

Finished size: Before felting, belly 48", body 15" from rim to center base. After felting, belly 29", body 10".

Stitch Guide: See page 112 for abbreviations, pages 110 - 111 for applied I-cord, page 109 for waste yarn and knitting with two circular needles, and page 108 for turning a Moebius band into a simple circle. *If using Cascade 220, work with 2 strands of yarn held together throughout.*

Begin with Moebius rim

With longer needle and main color, MCO 81 and set up with 3 half-twists as shown on page 96. Place marker. *Knit 1 round, p 1 round, repeat from * twice, k 1 last round. With contrast color, work applied I-cord until all sts are bound off. Graft or sew I-cord ends together.

Start bowl

Lay out rim as shown in photo on page 97. With shorter needle and main color, pick up sts in the charcoal purl bumps directly beneath the contrast color I-cord edge as follows: *Pick up 22 sts. Pick up 5 sts in the diagonally folded color band. Repeat from * twice. Place marker. (81 sts) Knit 1 round. *Knit 2, k1f&b, repeat from * to marker. (108 sts) Knit 10 rounds.

Base of bowl

You will need to change to 2 circular needles as the stitch count decreases.
*Knit 10, k2tog, repeat from * to marker. (99 sts) Knit 4 rounds. *Knit 9, k2tog, repeat from * to marker. (90 sts) Knit 4 rounds. *Knit 8, k2tog, repeat from * to marker. (81 sts) Knit 4 rounds. *Knit 7, k2tog, repeat from * to marker. (72 sts) Cut tail of yarn. With contrast color, p 4 rounds. Cut tail of yarn. With main color, *p 6, p2tog, repeat from * to marker. (63 sts) Purl 3 rounds. *Purl 5, p2tog, repeat from * to marker. (54 sts) Cut tail of yarn. With contrast color, p 3 rounds. *Purl 4, p2tog, repeat from * to marker. (45 sts) Purl 2 rounds. Cut tail of yarn. With main color, *p 3, p2tog, repeat from * to marker. (36 sts) Purl 1 round. *Purl 4, p2tog, repeat from * to marker. (30 sts) Purl 1 round. *Purl 3, p2tog, repeat from * to marker. (24 sts) Cut tail of yarn. With contrast color, p 1 round. *Purl 2tog, repeat from * to marker. (12 sts) Purl 1 round. *Purl 2tog, repeat from * to marker. (6 sts) Cut tail, thread through remaining sts, pull snug, and weave in securely.

Felting and finishing

Felt according to general instructions on pages 16-19. Agitate until thick and firm, then spin out the excess water. Place a sturdy small plate upside down in the bottom of the bowl, centering the rings on the plate. Place the bowl on the floor. Now step on the plate and shift enough of your weight to it to hold the base of the bowl flat and stable, while you pull and push and mold the sides into a nice round shape. Make sure to pull upward on the middle of each third of the rim, in between the crossings, so the bowl's height is greater here than at the crossings. Spread and stretch the rim out so that it resembles the photos. When satisfied, let dry.

SOMERSAULTING RIM TRIFOLD HAT

I apologize for not having a photo of this bowl worn as a hat, but it was only days before the book went to press that my delightful workshop students, at Knitopia in British Columbia, convinced me that this is a splendid hat. You may either wear it as is, which will make you a few inches taller, or fold the brim up for a shorter style. In either case, I recommend you actually let it slowly dry on your very own head, where it will take the shape that is you. A few hours of cranial communing with the damp hat ought to set the shape and size, and then you can fluff your hair back up. Everyone who puts this hat on immediately looks startlingly majestic.

TRIFOLD SANDSTONE & SKY BAG

You may recall the Sandstone & Sky Felted Stripes Moebius scarf from the first Treasury. Here is its sibling. The bag's stripes reveal the design's inherent trifold geometry, clearly visible in the flat unfelted form. The bag will hold a little or a lot, because of its ability to sink or swell. The I-cord straps, knit of one strand of each color held together, merge the colors, and are very loosely braided. It is a joyful bag.

Yarn: Lana Grossa Royal Tweed (100% Merino Fine, 50 g/ 100 m, 9 wpi), Sandstone and Sky, 3 skeins each

Needles: (you may require a different size to get correct gauge) size 10.5 (7 mm) circular, 47" - 55" length, also 16" - 24" length. Size 13 (9 mm) double pointed needles or a 16" circular in same size, for I-cord straps.

Notions: tapestry needle, three small double pointed needles to help pick up rim stitches, stitch markers

Gauge: (before felting) 14 sts = 4" (10 cm), using size 10.5 (7 mm) needles

Finished size: Before felting, circumference at widest point 44", height from bottom center to top of trifold rim 19", strap length 75". After felting, circumference 35", height 14", and braided straps 40".

Stitch Guide: See page 112 for abbreviations and page 109 for knitting with two circular needles.

Begin with trifold rim

With Sandstone, MCO 72 and set up with 3 half-twists as shown on page 96. Place marker. Knit 180 (1 full round of 144 plus a half-round of 36). Place new marker here, and remove first one when you come to it. *(You have established a new beginning point.)* Cut tail of Sandstone. With Sky, p 4 rounds. Cut tail of Sky. With Sandstone, k 4 rounds. Cut tail of Sandstone. With Sky, p 4 rounds. Cut tail of Sky. With Sandstone, *k25, bind off 6, k10, bind off 6, k1. Repeat from * twice. *Purl 25, cast on 6, p10, cast on 6, p1. Repeat from * twice. *Knit 1 round, p 1 round, repeat from * once. Bind off all sts and weave in ends.

Continue with bag

Change to the 16" needle and then to 2 circular needles as the stitch count decreases. You will pick up 24 sts along each diagonal section and 14 sts along each edge section. First arrange the trifold rim as shown on the next page. Use 3 double-pointed needles to pick up the 24 sts along each diagonal, as shown. Think of the openings as pairs of eyes, and arrange the trifold so that each pair of eyes is evenly spaced between the diagonal sides. Put one hand beneath the

trifold and poke a finger in one opening, then the other hand's finger in the visible opening to help you feel when they are balanced. Use 16" - 24" needle to pick up the 14 sts along each edge, and slip diagonal sts from the double pointed needles. When all 114 sts are picked up, place marker. With Sandstone, k 1 round. *Knit 2, k1f&b, repeat from * to marker. (152 sts). Knit 2 rounds. *Knit 4 rounds Sky, 4 rounds Sandstone, repeat from * once. With Sky, k2tog, k49, place marker, k2tog, k49, place marker, k50. (150 sts) *Knit until 3 sts before next marker, cdd, remove marker, k1, replace marker. Repeat from * twice. Knit 1 round. Repeat last two rounds until 6 sts remain. Cut tail, thread through remaining sts, pull snug, and weave in securely.

I-cord straps

Hold one strand of each color together. With 2 size 13 (9 mm) double-pointed needles, or one 16" size 13 circular, cast on 2 sts. *After each round push the sts to top of needle, pull yarn around back, and knit next round.* Round 1: Knit 2. Round 2: Knit 1, k 1 st in each strand of the next st. (3 sts). Round 3: Knit 1, k 1 in each strand of next st, k1. (4 sts). Continue knitting rounds of 4 sts until strap is 75" long. Knit 1, k2tog, k1. (3 sts). Knit 1, k2tog. (2 sts). Cut tail, thread through

remaining 2 sts, and sew both ends up through interior of strap. Make 2 additional 75" straps.

Felting and finishing

Felt according to general instructions on pages 16-19. But before felting, take a moment to enjoy the lovely geometry of the stripes, as shown below, because they will never look this way again. During the felting process, take the straps out early, when they are lightly felted. They should be narrower but not a great deal shorter. Wring out all three and then hold the ends together while you press your foot against the middles to stretch them all to the same length. Meanwhile, keep an eye on the bag which is still agitating. When you like the size and feel, stop the machine. Squeeze or spin out the excess water, and blow up a balloon in the bag to let it dry, or throw it in a warm dryer, checking every so often. Thread one strap through adjacent eyes, not the original pairs, but a right and a left from adjacent trifold petals. Holding all of the strap ends together, even them out, divide into two sets of three, and loosely braid each set. Tie pairs of ends in square knots. If you prefer, you may carefully cut and sew the ends together within the pattern of the braids, if you don't care for the knots.

This is what the bag looks like before felting. The other side has a single decrease line down the center. Both are beautiful!

TRIFOLD KNITTER'S BOWL

This handsome bowl, which revolves on a small lazy Susan, serves as a sort of knitter's carpenter's belt, although you do not wear it. Six pouches circle the edges, holding the tools you use daily: scissors, stitch markers, measuring tape, pen, calculator, glasses, and so on. Like an old-fashioned coin purse, three partial circles overlap to close off the top while still allowing free access, so you can put your yarn inside and pull a working strand without the ball popping out and rolling away to attract the attention of dust bunnies and those ever-alert felines. Three green I-cord crossings decoratively ring the Trifold band, and a trio of overlapping covers grows out of the three crossings like flower petals. This design evolved oganically, revealing its wonders to me bit by bit, like a little acorn which holds the secret of how to grow into a great oak tree. And now I've come to love having my Trifold Knitter's Bowl beside my chair, where it whirls around to put just what I need right at my fingertips. It reminds me of the old-fashioned carousel at the Fleischacker Zoo in San Francisco, where I used to ride a carved lion as a little girl. Now my knitting tools get to go for a well-deserved ride on their own magical carousel.

Yarn: Araucania Nature Wool (100% wool, 100 g/ 242 yds, 15 wpi), brown, 2 skeins; green, 1 skein; red, 1 skein; 6 pieces waste yarn

Needles: (you may require a different size to get correct gauge) size 11 (8 mm) circular, 47" – 60" length, also 24" and 16" length

Notions: tapestry needle, stitch markers, sturdy 12" plate or baking tin for blocking, small lazy Susan to hold the bowl and let it revolve

Gauge: (before felting, using 2 strands of yarn held together) 13 sts = 4" (10 cm)

Finished size: Before felting, rim is 2.5" wide and 36" around, belly 43" around, body 18" from rim to center base. After felting, rim is 1.75" wide and 26" around, belly 30", body 13".

Stitch Guide: See page 112 for abbreviations, page 110 - 111 for applied I-cord, page 109 for waste yarn and knitting with two circular needles, and page 108 for turning a Moebius band into a simple circle. *Knit with two strands of yarn held together throughout.*

Begin with Moebius rim

With longest needle and brown, MCO 99 and set up with 3 half-twists as shown on page 96. Place marker. *Knit 1 round, p 1 round, repeat from * twice. Knit 1 round. With green, work applied I-cord until all sts are bound off. Graft or sew I-cord ends together.

Start bowl and establish pouch openings

With 24" needle, pick up 99 sts directly beneath the rim's I-cord edge as follows: *Pick up 1 st in each row along the center of the I-cord for 27 sts, then pick up 6 sts in the diagonally folded brown band. Repeat from * twice. (99 sts). Knit 1 round. *Knit 1, k1f&b, repeat from *, end k1. (148 sts) Knit 1 round, increasing 2 sts somewhere on this round. (150 sts) Knit 1 round. Knit to 7 sts before the next 6-st section along a brown fold, place marker. *Knit 20 with waste yarn, replace on left needle, knit over the 20 waste yarn sts, k5, repeat from * 5 times. Continue knitting until sides are 4.5" from green I-cord.

Base of bowl

You will need to change to 2 circular needles as the stitch count decreases. *Knit 8, k2tog, repeat from * to marker. (135 sts) Knit 4 rounds. *Knit 7, k2tog, repeat from * to marker. (120 sts) Knit 4 rounds. *Knit 6, k2tog, repeat from * to marker. (105 sts) Knit 4 rounds. *Knit 5, k2tog, repeat from * to marker. (90 sts) Knit 4 rounds. *Knit 4, k2tog, repeat from * to marker. (75 sts)

Knit 4 rounds. *Knit 3, k2tog, repeat from * to marker. (60 sts) Knit 4 rounds. *Knit 2, k2tog, repeat from * to marker. (45 sts) Knit 2 rounds. *Knit 1, k2tog, repeat from * to marker. (30 sts) Knit 2 rounds. *Knit 2tog, repeat from * to marker. (15 sts) Knit 1 round. *Knit 2tog, repeat from *, end k1. (9 sts) Cut tail, thread through remaining sts, pull snug, and weave in securely.

Pouches

Take care to work with right side of bowl facing you. With 16" needle, pick up the 40 waste yarn sts held by one of the waste yarn sections, and remove waste yarn. With red, *pick up and k 1 st in corner, place marker, pick up and k second st in corner, k20, repeat from * once. (44 sts) Knit until pouch is 5" long. *Knit 1, ssk, k until 3 sts before next marker, k2tog, k1, repeat from * once. Repeat this round twice more. (32 sts) Close with 3-needle bind-off or bind off and sew bottom together. Repeat process for the remaining five pouches.

Important: Each eye-shaped cover section is worked *back and forth in short rows*.

First overlapping cover section

With brown and 24" needle, wrong side facing you and working from right to left, pick up and k 6 sts along the rim's diagonal fold, 29 sts at the base of the green I-cord, and 6 sts along the next diagonal fold. (41 sts) Turn work.

Picking up stitches for first cover section

Second overlapping cover section

With wrong side facing you, pick up and k 6 sts along the rim's diagonal fold, 29 sts at the base of the green I-cord, and (overlapping the first cover section) 6 sts along the next diagonal fold. (41 sts) Work cover section same as first.

Picking up stitches for second cover section

Slip 1, p23, turn. Sl1, k6, turn. Sl1, p8, turn. Sl1, k10, turn. Continue working short rows, adding 2 sts beyond gap each row, until only 1 st remains beyond gap at each side of needle. Sl1, p39, turn. Sl1, k40, turn. Sl1, p39, turn. Sl1, k38, turn. Sl1, p36, turn. Sl1, k34, turn. Continue working short rows, working 2 fewer sts each time until you end with sl1, k8, turn. Slip 1, p23, turn. Work applied I-cord to bind off all sts, then sew down ends of I-cord, securing both ends, and weave in yarn ends.

Picking up stitches for third cover section. One end of the needle is hidden.

Third overlapping cover section

With wrong side facing you, pick up and k 6 sts beneath first section (along the rim's diagonal fold), 29 sts at the base of the green I-cord, and (overlapping the second cover section) 6 sts along the next diagonal fold. (41 sts)
Work cover section same as first.

Felting and finishing

Felt according to general instructions on pages 16-19. Since confining a piece as large and complex as this inside a cloth bag while felting may cause it to felt unevenly, I recommend you let this one swim freely in your washing machine. Add a half dozen tennis balls to help bat things around. Check the progress every few minutes, tugging and pulling at the cover sections to keep them nicely shaped. As you can see below, the Knitter's Bowl shrinks to about 65% its original size when felted.

To block, place a sturdy 12" diameter plate or baking tin in the bottom of the damp Knitter's Bowl, and hold the plate down while pulling up on the sides. Standing on the plate while pulling up gives you a lot of leverage. Pull and smooth the pouches into pleasing shapes, and do the same with the cover sections. Set the Knitter's Bowl, loosely stuffed with dry towels, and with the plate still inside, on a rack to dry.

Knitter's Bowl, before felting

Knitter's Bowl, after felting, 65% of original size

Appendix

- *Sources*
- *Magical knitting techniques*
- *Abbreviations*

Sources

Island Wools

islandwools@rockisland.com
135 Spring Street,
Friday Harbor, WA 98250
360-370-KNIT

Island Wools is our island's much loved yarn shop, run by Julie Taylor. Take the ferry from Anacortes, and after the enchantment of sailing for a little more than an hour through emerald waters past countless small islands, you'll arrive on San Juan Island. Walk up the gentle hill and two minutes later you'll be surrounded by a scrumptious collection of yarn, buttons, books, and knitting tools. You can sit and knit in the adjacent sheltered courtyard, rain or shine. If you're looking for yarn raised and spun in the islands, inspiration, or a signed copy of one of my books, this is the place to go.

Krystal Acres Alpaca Farm

www.krystalacres.com
152 Blazing Tree Road
Friday Harbor, WA 98250
360-378-6125

I took some of the photos for this book at Krystal Acres, including this baby alpaca, who is eying a Jester Tentacles Bag. The farm is open for visitors.

Westcott Bay Reserve for Art & Nature

www.wbay.org (on San Juan Island)
I took the picture on page 34 at this seaside sculpture park and nature reserve, which is an extraordinary place to explore for a few hours.

Cascade Yarns

www.cascadeyarns.com
Cascade offers your local yarn shop a painter's palette (over 200 colors) of fabulous felting yarns. I particularly love Cascade 220 and Pastaza.

Crystal Palace Yarns

www.straw.com
You'll find their delicious yarns in both *Treasuries*, and their classic bamboo circular knitting needles come in a 55" length, just perfect for Moebius knitting. Their Iceland yarn is ideal for thickly felted creations, like cat beds and Trifold Bowls.

Denise Needle Kits

888-831-8042   www.knitdenise.com
When you are knitting a Moebius bowl, basket, or bed, and decreasing away as you aim for the closure, you'll be glad you have a Denise Needle Kit close by. With their nifty set of connectors and various cable lengths, you can replace your cable with a shorter one in seconds and keep knitting with scarcely a pause. See pages 10 and 97 for a second trick, and their web site for details on other practical stunts they can perform.

Knitknack

www.knitknack.com
Purveyors of tantalizing handmade knitting needles, topped with anthracite coal, cinnabar, pearls, silver, and more.

Fleece Artist

www.fleeceartist.com
These yarns from Cape Breton Island in Nova Scotia shimmer with color, texture, and radiance. You'll find them primarily in Canada. Island Wools (see listing) is one of the few and fortunate U.S. vendors.

Philosopher's Wool

www.philosopherswool.com
Eugene and Ann Bourgeois support their local farmers by turning their fleeces into wonderful yarn. And if you want to learn the best ever method for weaving strands in two-color knitting, check out the short video on their web site, or buy their book to learn this and much more.

Russi Sales, Inc.

www.russisales.com
Distributors of Chuckanut Bay Yarn, used in the Somersaulting Rim Trifold Bowl. This yarn is superb for felted bowls, baskets, bags, and cat beds, and comes in generous skeins.

The Skacel Collection, Inc.

www.skacelknitting.com
Skacel provides yarn shops with the sleek and wonderful Addi Turbo circular needles, which come in Turbo finish brass or bamboo tips, and in three Moebius sizes (40" for hats, 47" for almost everything, and 60" for really bulky yarn), as well as the India yarn used in the Cinnamon Braid Sling Bag and Rolled Edge Sling Bag.

Louet Sales

www.louet.com
Makers of Euroflax Linen.

Unicorn Books & Crafts, Inc.

www.unicornbooks.com
Unicorn's Lana Grossa Royal Tweed Yarn, lightly felted, creates the most remarkable fabric, reminiscent of an expensive camel hair throw from the good old days. I used it for the Trifold Sandstone & Sky Bag, the matching Moebius scarf from the first *Treasury*, and the Spacious Show & Tell Moebius Bag.

Wool in the Woods

www.woolinthewoods.com
Best friends Anita Tostens and Missy Burns are more fun than a barrel of monkeys and run a wonderful hand-dyed yarn business. With Stephanie Blaydes Kaisler, they've written a book, *Knitting With Hand-Dyed Yarns: 20 Stunning Projects,* as well. I used their hand-dyed Sophia in several Moebius Bowls and Star City Wool in the Spacious Desert Sunrise Bag.

Gifted Hands

www.giftedhandsknits.com
Creators of Pixie Sticks knitting needles, with swirly tops to match the spiral needle cozies.

Knitting Fever

www.knittingfever.com
Distributors of Araucania yarns.

Robert J. Lang Origami

www.langorigami.com
Robert Lang knows his way around a Moebius as well as any living person, and miraculously folds zero-volume Klein bottles (a Moebius relative) with one sheet of paper and no cuts. On his site you'll find a wonderland of creatures so beautiful and true to life, you will gasp.

Cat teaching a Moebius design workshop at Knitopia, an aptly named knitter's utopia in White Rock, British Columbia, just five minutes from the Douglas (Peace Arch) border crossing. Phone for directions: (604) 531-4818.

Antoinette Botsford, PhD

storybird@rockisland.com

All of Antoinette's stories have at their movable center something as supple and slippery as a Moebius and as certain to echo in your soul. If you'd like her to tell you stories while you knit your Moebius, you may email her (see above) for information on her three CD's of stories.

Vanessa Rose Ament

www.vanessaroseament.com

One day Vanessa will have a CD available, and the walls of your heart will dissolve in the sheer liquid beauty of her voice. In the meantime, check her web site to find out if she is performing near you.

Cat Bordhi

web site: *www.catbordhi.com*
email: *cat@catbordhi.com*

Visit Cat's web site for her workshop schedule, free patterns, and information about evolving discoveries or projects that may show up in new books and workshops. If you find mistakes in this book, please let her know! She will post them on the web site, and correct them in future editions.

TECHNIQUES

A Moebius band becomes a simple circle

You'll use this technique when picking up stitches along the base of a Moebius rim to begin knitting a bowl, basket, or bed.

This Moebius band has one half its stitches bound off. The remaining stitches are about to join in a simple circle. The lower needle will rise up to meet the upper needle.

The stitches are now lined up in a simple circle. If you have too few stitches for the needle, like I do here, switch to a shorter one. Now you can knit downwards, to make a bowl, basket, or bed.

This is Ben, a real live knitted boy, and the main character in my novel, Treasure Forest. *He is holding his needle quiver, ready to knit a tree house in the forest. Ben was born before the novel, and became my co-author. I did not record how I made him, because after all, he is real. He is wearing his Moebius scarf and a Tomten Jacket (an Elizabeth Zimmermann design).*

Knitting with Two Circular Needles

To knit with 2 circular needles, place half the stitches on each needle. The working needle ignores the resting  needle, knits its own stitches, then rests while the other needle knits its own stitches.

I am holding the ends of the working needle (which is in front). The other needle (which is in back) is resting  quietly with its stitches, like a stitch holder.

Once the first needle finishes knitting its stitches, the yarn has moved into place for the second needle to use. When that needle finishes knitting its stitches, the first needle takes the yarn. And around and around they go, like a team of relay runners, handing off the baton to each other as they circle the track, only in this case they are handing the working yarn to each other.

Here I have knit halfway across the first needle. See the second needle resting below? When I finish knitting across the first needle, the second needle will wake up, take the yarn, and get to work, while the first needle rests. They keep taking turns working and resting.

Waste yarn openings

This technique allows you to pop open your knitting to add a pouch, bowl, pocket, or tentacle.

Drop the working yarn and knit a section of stitches with waste yarn. Then put all the waste yarn stitches back on the left needle (as shown).

Now the working yarn knits right over the waste yarn stitches, treating them like ordinary stitches.

The waste yarn stitches are now sandwiched between two rows of working stitches.

Picking up waste yarn stitches

When you turn over the knitting, you see each stitch held in a waste yarn loop. Pick up each row of stitches with a needle. Many knitters find it easiest to pick up each row with a separate needle, but it can be  done with one circular needle as well. A smaller needle makes things easier. Remove the waste yarn, and knit the picked up stitches with your working yarn.

Applied I-Cord

First add 2 stitches with a knitted cast-on

Step 1: Knit 1 stitch but do not move the completed stitch to the right needle as you normally would.

Step 2: Slip the new stitch onto the left needle. Twist the stitch before slipping it over the left needle tip.

Step 3: Knit 1 stitch in the twisted stitch on your left needle tip, but do not move the completed stitch to the right needle.

Step 4: Instead, slip it onto the left needle tip, twisting it as in step 2. You now have 2 new stitches on your left needle, both twisted.

You have done the Knitted Cast-On, and set yourself up to start the Applied I-Cord.

Step 5: Knit 3 stitches.

Step 6: Replace the 3 sts you just knit back onto the left needle. Your working yarn is coming from the back of the 3rd stitch.

Step 7: Knit 2 stitches, pulling the yarn up from the bottom of the 3rd stitch.

Step 8: Knit the next 2 sts together from right to left, through the back loops.

Repeat steps 6-8 until all stitches are bound off.

You can graft the I-cord ends together, as shown on the next page, or bind off and sew the ends together.

Grafting I-cord ends

Step 1: Insert knitting needle at I-cord beginning, through a row of 3 knit stitches. Cut a tail of working yarn and thread it through a tapestry needle.

Step 2: Insert tapestry needle through first loop on lower needle as if to purl. Pull yarn through.

Step 3: Insert tapestry needle through first loop on upper needle as if to knit. Pull yarn through.

Step 4: Insert tapestry needle behind next 2 loops on lower needle. Pull yarn through.

Step 5: Insert tapestry needle through first loop on upper needle as if to purl, and take loop off needle. Pull yarn through.

Step 6: Insert tapestry needle through next loop on upper needle as if to knit. Pull yarn through.

Repeat steps 4 - 6

Step 7: Remove upper needle, and insert tapestry needle through last stitch on lower needle from left to right. Pull yarn through. Remove lower needle.

Step 8: Insert tapestry needle through final edge stitch that was on upper needle, as if to purl. Pull yarn through.

Step 9: Insert tapestry needle through final edge stitch that was on lower needle. Pull yarn through. Give the join a tug to pull the stitches neatly into alignment. Weave in the tail.

To graft wider I-cord (with more than 3 stitches) repeat steps 4 - 6 once more for each extra stitch.

ABBREVIATIONS

cdd (centered double decrease) Insert right needle into next 2 sts as if you were going to work k2tog (through both from left to right). Slip the sts to the right needle. Knit the next st on the left needle. Pass the slipped sts over the st you just knit.

k knit

k1f&b knit through front and back of same stitch

k2tog knit 2 stitches together

MCO (Moebius Cast-On) Instructions begin on page 10. This cast-on is the entry point to the whole Magical Knitting collection.

p purl

p1f&b purl through front and back of same stitch

p2tog purl 2 stitches together

p3tog purl 3 stitches together

ssk (slip, slip, knit) With yarn in back, separately slip 1 st and then the next as if to knit (this changes their mounts). Put them back on left needle and knit together through back loops, from right to left.

st(s) stitches

tbl through back loop

wpi wraps per inch
To determine wraps per inch of any yarn, wrap it around a ruler, push strands together so they touch, and count how many strands line up side by side in one inch. Wraps per inch is a good way to compare yarn when substituting. You'll find wraps per inch information in every pattern, so you can easily substitute.